Methods of Teaching

TEACHER TRAINING

Methods of Teaching
TEACHER TRAINING

Dr. T. Shankar

CRESCENT
PUBLISHING CORPORATION

[*The responsibility for the facts stated, conclusions reached and plagiarism, if any, in this book is entirely that of the Author. And the Publisher bears no responsibility for them, whatsoever.*]

Methods of Teaching Teacher Training

First Published : 2015

ISBN 81-8342-060-5

Published by :

CRESCENT PUBLISHING CORPORATION
4831/24, Prahlad Street,
Ansari Road, Darya Ganj,
New Delhi - 110002
Ph. : 23272541, 23257835
Fax : 91- 011- 23257835
e-mail : campusbooks@hotmail.com

Printed at :
Roshan Offset Printers
Delhi

Methods of Teaching
TEACHER TRAINING

Dr. T. Shankar

CRESCENT
PUBLISHING CORPORATION

[*The responsibility for the facts stated, conclusions reached and plagiarism, if any, in this book is entirely that of the Author. And the Publisher bears no responsibility for them, whatsoever.*]

Methods of Teaching Teacher Training

First Published : 2015

ISBN 81-8342-060-5

Published by :

CRESCENT PUBLISHING CORPORATION
4831/24, Prahlad Street,
Ansari Road, Darya Ganj,
New Delhi - 110002
Ph. : 23272541, 23257835
Fax : 91- 011- 23257835
e-mail : campusbooks@hotmail.com

Printed at :
Roshan Offset Printers
Delhi

Preface

Teacher training is a topic that has not attracted the attention it deserves, at least until recently. Now it is becoming clear that despite all the teacher training, credentialing, and annual evaluations that teachers have undergone for years, there are enormous differences in effectiveness among fully qualified and experienced teachers. These differences reflect the education community's view that student achievement is not public education's highest priority. Rather, achievement is only one valued outcome among many, and it often suffers from inattention.

The pedagogical concepts in which teachers are indoctrinated shape the education community's preference for schooling that is relatively ineffective and inefficient. Teacher training has to suit the needs and demands of the modern world. Many countries have realised the need for redefining teachers' roles and have responded by launching innovative teacher training programmes. But there are enormous problems while applying the new methods of teacher training.

This book describes the problems and methods of teacher training. It explores the shortcomings of teacher education and proposes design principles for rethinking teacher preparation. It is hoped that this book will prove useful to teaching departments and institutions, teachers of educational administrations and all those concerned.

Dr. T. Shankar

Preface

Teacher training is a topic that has not attracted the attention it deserves, at least until recently. Now it is becoming clear that despite all the teacher training, credentialing, and annual evaluations that teachers have undergone for years, there are enormous differences in effectiveness among fully qualified and experienced teachers. These differences reflect the education community's view that student achievement is not public education's highest priority. Rather, achievement is only one valued outcome among many, and it often suffers from inattention.

The pedagogical concepts in which teachers are indoctrinated shape the education community's preference for schooling that is relatively ineffective and inefficient. Teacher training has to suit the needs and demands of the modern world. Many countries have realised the need for redefining teachers' roles and have responded by launching innovative teacher training programmes. But there are enormous problems while applying the new methods of teacher training.

This book describes the problems and methods of teacher training. It explores the shortcomings of teacher education and proposes design principles for rethinking teacher preparation. It is hoped that this book will prove useful to teaching departments and institutions, teachers of educational administrations and all those concerned.

Dr. T. Shankar

Contents

1

Introduction to Teacher Training

Good education demands good teachers. But many countries have too few teachers, or teachers who have themselves had only a limited, or outdated education. At the same time, the development of open and distance learning, and the promises held out by new information and communication technologies, suggest that there may be new ways of expanding the teaching service and raising its quality.

The curriculum of teacher education may be dominated be one or other element, from general education to classroom skills, and varies in the emphasis it places on pre-service and in service approaches. Within different jurisdictions, responsibility for it may be shared among ministries of education, universities, curriculum agencies, and teachers' colleges.

At the time of the 2000 World Conference on Education for All there were some 113 million children outside school. Even when the targets agreed at the conference are achieved, 'success in improving access and quality at the primary education level leads to increased demand for post-primary education and for teacher training'. At the same time there is more than 40 years experience of programmes to expand teacher supply, and raise the quality of teachers in schools, through the use of distance education. New communication technologies have been seen as a way of strengthening the use of distance education.

Throughout much of the south and especially in sub-Saharan Africa and south Asia, problems of teacher supply, of three kinds, threaten the attainment of the education targets.

First, there are shortages of teachers. While school enrolments generally grew in the 1990s, teacher numbers only just kept pace with them, while AIDS is reducing the life expectancy of teachers and so increasing the numerical demands. With all the other pressures on educational budgets, it seems unlikely that teachers' colleges can be expanded at the rate necessary to meet these demands. Morbidity as well as mortality is affecting the teaching service: where teachers are too ill to work, their absence worsens teacher shortages.

Second, in the same two regions, female teachers are in a minority. Progress in getting more women into the profession is slow; in Africa the proportion of women primary school teachers rose from 39.4 percent to 43.3 per cent between 1990 and 1997, while in south Asia it rose only from 28.0 to 29.6 per cent. Where tradition, religion or social pressure means that only women can teach girls, these figures threaten the attainment of both the world targets.

Third, even where there are enough teachers, too many of them are untrained or under trained, and the quality of training is often itself inadequate. A number of studies have found little difference between the effectiveness of trained and untrained teachers. 'About half of the teachers in developing countries are unqualified in terms of their own country's formal standards for teachers' education. Many teachers have little more than secondary education themselves.

Teaching methods are often old fashioned, with too much focus on rote learning'. Problems of quality are compounded by a growing concern to reform education and change the role of the teacher: many countries wish not just to raise the quality of the teaching force to match the present demands on them but also to change the nature of those demands.

Responsibilities for Teacher Education and Training

Responsibility for teacher education is often shared among different stakeholders while influence over its content and methods may be shared even more widely. Ministries of education most often have primary responsibility for teacher education. In many cases this responsibility may be devolved or shared. Where a teaching service commission exists, it may have some responsibility for teacher education and for the recognition of qualifications. Curriculum agencies are likely to have an interest in and possibly a responsibility for teacher education and training. In some cases, and especially in large or federal countries, some responsibilities and activities are devolved.

In India, for example, District Institutes for Education and Training (DIETs) have a major role in both the pre-service and the continuing education of teachers. Ministries, too, have a financial concern for teacher education: not only are teachers' colleges generally funded from the ministry budget but any programmes that raise the level of qualification of teachers are likely to have a long-term impact on teachers' salaries, the biggest item in a ministry budget.

Teachers' colleges may be controlled by a ministry of education, or have a degree of autonomy, or be seen as belonging with universities in a tertiary sector of education. Their organisational location may change over the years. They have sometimes had a difficult and unrewarding link with distance-education programmes, where these were seen as being in competition with their regular, and more conventional work. Where a distance-education programme needs to use the facilities of teachers' colleges then good relationships between the two are at a premium.

Universities may have a variety of different links with and responsibilities for teacher education. In some cases these include monitoring and accreditation; teacher education in Belize and Jamaica, for example, is supervised and accredited by a Joint Board for Teacher Education based at the University of the West Indies. Some teacher education programmes are run directly by universities and open universities in particular have often been called on by governments to use their skills in distance education to run programmes for teachers: the ministry of education in Pakistan, for example, has used the facilities of Allama Iqbal Open University to meet the need for continuing education of the country's serving primary school teachers. Thus universities may have different roles as an accrediting agency, as the implementer of programmes that rely on the expertise of its own faculty of education, and as the provider of specialist skills in distance education.

Teacher education is likely to have a twofold relationship with schools, at once influencing them and reacting to them. Short periods of teaching practice will take the students and may take the staff of teachers' colleges into schools. Where schools are responsible for mentoring trainee teachers, as happened with the postgraduate certificate course of the Open University in Britain, they become directly involved in teacher education. While this involvement may reduce the likelihood of conflict between teachers' college and school, it has also been criticised as weakening an opportunity of changing school culture through external influence.

The concerns of individual teachers will be reflected by their schools but may also be expressed by teachers' unions and professional associations, both nationally and internationally. Good policy planning will take their interests into account; many have been warmly supportive of measures that can be seen as raising the status and widening the opportunities of their members. International agencies may in turn influence teacher education and the use of distance education within it. Both the Commonwealth of Learning and its franco phone equivalent, CIFFAD, have been involved in the development of teacher education programmes using distance education, and have been able to share expertise internationally in their execution.

A project in Burkina Faso to train head teachers, for example, could call on resources elsewhere in west Africa and in France through the network RESAFAD (Réseau africain de formation à distance or African network for distance education). The World Bank has sought to influence policy on teacher education while several bilateral aid agencies in Europe have funded distance-education projects for teachers in Africa. They have brought to their funding their own policy concerns as well as their cash. The complexity of this web of responsibility and influence—a complexity that is inherent in the use of distance education—means that it is sometimes difficult to see who has a sense of ownership of teacher education.

In India, for example, one programme for primary school teachers was executed by Indira Gandhi National Open University, on behalf of the ministry of education, in association with a national curriculum agency, the National Council for Educational Research and Training, and with responsibility for accreditation and monitoring resting with the National Board for Teacher Education. For the policy maker one conclusion is clear, and easy to state while demanding in practice: identify the stakeholders and create as simple mechanisms as possible to encourage their collaboration.

Pupose of Teacher Education and Training

Teacher education and training has to respond to the demands of the various stakeholders and therefore to do a number of different jobs. There are expectations that it will enable teachers to develop the potential of their pupils; help them serve as role models; transform education and through it society; develop changed attitudes to their work and to education; and encourage their own self-confidence and creativity. The curriculum of any teacher-education programme will be shaped by local needs and by the programme's purpose; the planner's first question is therefore about purpose.

There are two starting distinctions: between the initial education and training of teachers and their continuing professional development, and between pre-service and in service activities. The two sets of distinctions do not overlap: many teachers begin work without teaching qualifications so that they may get initial training while they are working in service. Beyond those initial distinctions we can differentiate between programmes designed to support curriculum development and those to help teachers undertake a new role, often to work in administration or in a teachers' college.

In practice, some of these distinctions may be blurred: programmes to support a changed curriculum may be directed at all teachers, regardless of their earlier training. In Pakistan, for example, a Primary Teachers Orientation Course was run in the interests of curriculum reform but served also as continuing professional development for many teachers and, in practice, as initial training for unqualified teachers already working in the service. Many programmes of teacher education—and especially those that are providing initial training—include four elements: improving the general educational background of the trainee teachers; increasing their knowledge and understanding of the subjects they are to teach; pedagogy and understanding of children and learning; and the development of practical skills and competences. The balance between these four elements varies in relation to the background education of student teachers, to the level at which they will teach, and to the stage they have reached in their career.

Table 1. Purposes of teacher education programmes

Purposes	subcategories
Initial training of unqualified teachers	programmes leading to certification short induction courses
Upgrading of teachers who already have a qualification	for subqualified teachers for qualified teachers
Training related to content of the school curriculum	for planned curriculum change refresher courses
Preparing teachers for new roles	as head teachers to work in teachers' colleges

Beyond this, the curriculum of teacher education is likely to be shaped by the circumstances of trainee teachers and by changes in prevailing attitudes to education or shifts in educational philosophy. In considering teachers' own circumstances we need to take account of: their educational background, which varies enormously between different countries and different levels of education. gender, where there are shortages of women teachers in many countries, and of men teachers in some. Programmes need to fit with the rest of teachers' lives and be sensitive to cultural norms and expectations that affect their jobs.

In some countries there are restrictions on women teachers' mobility that affect their ability to attend initial or updating courses. their experience as teachers where trainees who have just left school with limited formal education are likely to have quite different educational needs from those with similar formal qualifications but long experience as untrained teachers. In many countries teacher education gives an impression of rethinking, and restructuring of the curriculum, although it is often unclear how far this process has changed actual practice. One change has been a shift of emphasis from pre-service to in service education. At either stage a recurrent picture is the coexistence of traditional and newer curriculum models within one programme. This takes the form of two competing strands of thinking that, for convenience, can be labelled as traditional and progressive tendencies.

The traditional is teacher centred, based on behaviourist assumptions, has a transmission view of knowledge and regards the teacher as a technician; the progressive strand includes more active and participatory learning methods, is less authoritarian, places more demands on teachers and contains elements of constructivist thinking. The progressive agenda encourages the development of reflective practice among teachers. This in turn raises questions about the practicality of rapid change and the danger, identified by Beeby in a classic analysis of seeking over-rapid transformation and of holding unrealistic expectations of teachers who were themselves teaching at the limit of their knowledge.

Thus the planner needs to ask how far it is realistic to ask trainee teachers to adopt new roles and carry them out effectively on the basis of a limited educational background. Where programmes are available in parallel, at conventional colleges and at a distance, distance-education teacher trainees tend to have a lower educational background than those at regular residential teacher colleges. They are often older, have more practical teaching experience and include higher proportions of women who are trying to balance family commitments with part time study. Distance education may have a particular role here in widening educational opportunities to people and to areas with an entrenched history of educational deprivation.

Costs of Teacher Education Programme

Once the aims of a particular programme of teacher education have been articulated it is possible to ask how far distance education may be useful in meeting them and how it should be planned and organised. The planner's questions here are about the trade-offs between conventional and distance-education approaches. Distance education may have advantages in terms of access, scale, speed and cost. In principle it can reach students at any distance and, by reaching large audiences, provide in service education to teachers more rapidly than would be possible through conventional means. In some circumstances, the cost per student is likely to be lower than the cost for conventional, face-to-face, programmes, especially where these require student residence with all its associated costs. On the other hand, at least some aspects of teacher education are about human interactions and mediated education, done through print or broadcast or computer, may be an inappropriate methodology.

But there is a threefold case to be made for its legitimacy. First, the evidence of public-sector open universities, and dual-mode universities that teach both conventionally and at a distance, is that students can achieve examination results that match those of conventional universities. A significant proportion of students give up along the way and do not complete their courses. But this is true of all students working part-time and not a distinguishing mark of students learning at a distance. Second, distance education has been powerfully effective in reaching audiences who could not meet their educational needs from conventional institutions.

In Colombia, a radio-based school was, in the 1970s, reaching over 100,000 rural peasant students every year. The National Technological University in the United States is using satellite and broadcasting technology to meet the needs of engineers for postgraduate study without their having to leave their jobs and attend a campus. In China, the combined use of television, classroom sessions, and printed materials is providing university education to about a third of all the students in higher education. A church-based nongovernment organisation, the American private sector, and the government authorities in China have all perceived distance education as legitimate because of its power to widen access to education.

The policy maker's judgment will be influenced by evidence on outcomes and on costs. The evidence on outcomes is not as solid as we would like, reflecting the shortage of good research on the outcomes of teacher education generally. Several developing-country studies have found little difference in terms of classroom effectiveness between qualified and unqualified teachers. Few distance-education projects have followed trainee teachers into the classroom in order to see if their training made them better teachers. Where they have, notably in Tanzania and Zimbabwe the evidence shows that, while direct comparisons between teachers taught in different ways are difficult, the classroom practice of teachers' taught at a distance stood up comparatively well.

There is fuller evidence on three other indicators—of the number of students reached by programmes, on completion rates, and on examination results or learning gains. Many programmes have reached large numbers of students; Tanzania trained 38,000 teachers at a distance in the 1970s; China uses television based distance education for teachers numbered in the millions; Pakistan and Nigeria have used distance education for teacher audiences of 80,000 and 180,000 respectively. Where trainee teachers have been enrolled en bloc in a training programme, with a guarantee of improved qualifications and status on successfully compieting the course, completion rates have tended to be high.

Lower completion rates are reported where training amounts to secondary equivalence (in Nigeria) and in a number of cases where students have enrolled individually on courses without any guarantee of direct financial benefit. In terms of examination passes, a review of nine earlier case studies found that pass rates were between 50 and 90 per cent and argued that 'while examination success cannot be equated with teaching capacity, we can legitimately assume that a reasonable examination pass rate demonstrates that a programme was effective in teaching academic subjects'. Rather than look at examination results, we might want to ask how well trainee teachers learned.

Teacher education projects in Indonesia and Sri Lanka set out to measure this and found reasonable evidence of effectiveness that is in line with the evidence on examination results. A number of studies have made broad comparisons between the costs of training teachers conventionally and face-to-face. While these comparisons are necessarily crude, they consistently show that, with the relatively high completion rates often achieved in teacher education, costs per successful student tend to compare favourably with those of conventional education. This differential holds true both for projects with quite modest costs per student, reflecting limited student support, as in Pakistan, and those with relatively high costs incurred for extensive student support and supervision of classroom practice, as in Tanzania.

The actual cost per distance-education student, or cost per successful student, is a function of a number of factors of which the most significant are the scale of the number of enrolments, the amount of face-to-face support provided, and the sophistication of the technologies used. In looking at the comparative cost effectiveness of conventional and distance-education approaches, some of the most important differences flow from the fact that distance education is nonresidential, often part-time, and allows learners to work and study at the same time. This in turn has led to differences in policy about funding and in the opportunity costs of studying.

In considering options, the planner is likely to seek information and base decisions on:

- — the scale of the programmes;
- — the media or technologies used;
- — the costs of face-to-face or residential study;
- — the cost of other student support;
- — the costs of teaching practice and of supervising or examining it;
- — policy on charging fees; the opportunity costs of taking teachers out of school for their own education.

Organisational Management in Open and Distance Learning

Programmes and projects vary widely in the extent to which they are structured. At one extreme, the BBC, along with other public-service broadcasters, puts out broadcasts for teachers both nationally and internationally. They are intended to provide continuing education for teachers but without any requirement on teachers to enrol, or take part in any formal activity in relation to them. With a slightly more formal structure, the A-Plus programme in Brazil consists of a television series for teachers combined with optional sessions in teachers' centres that teachers can attend if they want to follow up ideas in the broadcasts. In other, more formally structured programmes, teachers enrol on a course which is taught, by print or broadcast or computer, and are required to submit assignments and study regularly, much as if they were enrolled on a conventional face-to-face course.

The National Teachers' Institute in Nigeria, for example, enrols students this way so that they have a route to becoming qualified teachers without attending a conventional college. While the main focus of this policy guide is on structured and semi-structured approaches, this is not meant to undervalue unstructured and nonformal approaches; the need for the guide follows from the complexity of the management issues involved in structured approaches. The convenience of broadcasting, and the increasing availability of making materials available on the internet, suggest that these approaches may be of major value to many teachers. Unfortunately the shortage of research studies means we have all too little data on the impact of unstructured programmes.

An analysis of the functions needed to make open and distance learning work is necessary in order to inform the choice between administrative options. To make distance education work you need structures and facilities for seven main functions. A range of different organisational structures have been used for teacher education at a distance which can be classified under as follows:

Ad-hoc Arrangements

In some cases a ministry of education has set up a project directly, making ad-hoc arrangements for all the necessary functions. While this approach may harness resources rapidly, it has not usually proved sustainable beyond a short-term emergency.

Single or Dual-mode Teachers' College

More often, prime responsibility rests with a teachers' college, often teaching conventionally as well as at a distance. Within the small country of Belize, the one teacher-training college developed a part-time distance version of its conventional initial teacher education programme, drawing on existing faculty members to develop materials and train those who were to be responsible for classroom supervision and marking assignments. Nigeria has a National Teachers Institute which is a single-purpose institution, teaching entirely through open and distance learning.

Single or Dual-Mode Universities

Universities may have two relevant areas of expertise—in the content of teacher education, where this is a university responsibility, and in the practice of open and distance learning. While it may be possible to benefit from either of these areas of expertise, there are sometimes problems of fit and adjustment if a university has no experience, in, say, the education of primary-school teachers which has generally been the responsibility of non-university teachers' colleges. Dual-mode universities have also often faced practical difficulties in developing teaching materials, mainly because of competing pressures on staff time.

Universities have run supply-led and demand-led programmes. In some instances ministries of education have turned to a university to supply a national programme because it has the infrastructure for materials development and distribution. In other cases, a university has responded to demand from teachers by developing courses relevant to their continuing professional development. Indira Gandhi National Open University in India, for example, runs programmes on which students enrol individually, paying their own fees, in order to raise the level of their qualifications.

Multicountry Programmes

There is limited, but growing, experience of programmes that go across frontiers. In franco phone Africa, RESAFAD has been working on projects to develop resources that can be shared across frontiers. The regional universities in the West Indies and the South Pacific have responsibilities in teacher education. The European Commission has supported a European-wide agreement on the content and certification of information and communication technologies in schools while the Commonwealth of Learning has designed a co-operative programme for teachers and administrators in eight southern African countries.

Nongovernment Organisations

Some nongovernment organisations have played a part in teacher education at a distance, either in parallel with or linked with the public education service. With external, donor, funding the Open Learning Systems Education Trust (OLSET) in South Africa, for example, is offering training for teachers in the context of its radio programme for schools. Nongovernment organisations have played a particularly strong role where, as in Latin America, a pluralist tradition assumes they have a major role in public education.

Consortia and Partnerships

In many cases, it will not be possible for any one institution to carry out all the functions needed for open and distance learning; instead they have to be shared between several partners. An open university, for example, may be contracted by a ministry of education for the development and central management of a programme but this is likely also to involve coordination or cooperation with any national accrediting agency, with curriculum bodies and possibly with public or private-sector broadcasting organisations. Cooperation with local colleges of education may be necessary for the supervision and management of the practical side of teacher education.

The idea of partnerships has been driven by three forces: the shift towards decentralisation, an increase in school-based teacher education, and decisions to integrate distance education and conventional approaches. While the benefits of partnerships are obvious, they present management difficulties and as might be expected, have functioned with varying degrees of success. The complexity, time and cost of managing these crucial relationships with partners tend to be underestimated at the outset, especially when several colleges and regional or district authorities are involved. Furthermore, consistency of quality is not easy to achieve in large geographically dispersed programmes with decentralised field operations, which also need to be responsive to local conditions. Problems in managing the system revolve around issues of responsibility, role definition, accountability, location of decision-making, communication and the control and co-ordination of part time support staff.

Teaching Practice

No matter which organisational option is chosen, decisions will be needed about the management, supervision and often assessment of teaching practice. This presents logistical difficulties in any programme of teacher education and these are likely to be magnified for large-scale programmes and scattered student audiences. Some projects and programmes have avoided the issue. Where, for example, the aim is to raise the general education of teachers then it may be legitimate not to worry about their classroom practice. But where programmes aim to have a direct influence on teachers' classroom practice then the issue needs to be addressed.

In India, Indira Gandhi National Open University's certificate programme was for experienced teachers and was about counselling rather than classroom activity. In Belize micro teaching was used as a substitute for classroom visits. Where these are arranged they may be combined in a separate block—perhaps simpler administratively or integrated with the rest of the course—encouraging links between theory and practice. There are examples of the use of school-based mentors to supervise classroom work.

For the manager, the simplest arrangement is to avoid any element of teaching practice, or to centralise arrangements as in the Belize example. But, where programmes are intended to have a direct influence on teachers' classroom practice, there is an imperative to supervise and monitor this. In many countries the third or fourth model has been adopted so that staff from the distance teaching institution or one of its partners visit teachers in their individual classrooms. Costs and logistics make this a difficult option but it is often the only realistic one.

The fifth model, of employing school-based mentors has attracted widespread interest. It needs teachers within the system who have themselves sufficient experience and understanding of education to act as mentors, as well as a structure to brief and train them and to monitor their work. In many developing countries, ministries of education conclude that these conditions cannot be met. It has also been criticised as a system which serves to replicate the existing culture and values of the schools where the mentors and their trainee teachers are working.

Impact of New Information and Communication Technology

In principle, distance educators may be able to choose from a wide range of technologies, from print to broadcasting to a variety of applications of computer based information and communication technologies. In practice the choice is likely to be constrained by practicalities and costs, as well as by educational purpose. As a starting point the planner needs to consider how far the institution and the learner both have access to a particular technology: broadcasting, for example, may look attractive to the planner but is no use if most students are outside the range of a transmitter or broadcasting time is available only at inappropriate hours. Information about costs may be next in importance, as technologies vary in their costs and their cost behaviour.

The most significant difference in behaviour is between costs where economies of scale are possible, such as radio, and those where they are negligible, such as face-to-face tutoring or marking individual assignments. In choosing technologies it is also necessary to distinguish between their two main functions of distributing teaching material and allowing interaction between tutor and student. Again, economies are more likely to be available in distribution, where it costs no more to broadcast to a thousand students than a hundred, than in interaction. The division between the two functions is usually clear-cut. Radio, for example, is a one-way medium which can only distribute teaching to learners while telephone tutoring, or face-to-face meetings, allow interaction.

The new information and communication technologies provide the single main exception to this rule; if students have internet access then it can be used both to distribute teaching material to them and as a means of two-way communication. One consequence of this is likely to be a reduction in the institution's costs and an increase in the student's, where responsibility for reproducing printed matter is shifted from the institution to the learner. But this is very much the exception: more often the planner needs to balance the advantages of, say, broadcasting against print as media for distribution and face-to-face against written opportunities for feedback from students.

There is no simple match between educational purpose and technology. Generally, there is a case for using more than one technology in open and distance learning, partly because this is likely to be more interesting for the learner, partly as an insurance policy (if the mail does not get through the broadcast may), partly because there may be educational advantages in using one medium rather than another (audio tapes have an advantage over print in teaching the pronunciation of a language). This in turn may drive a teaching institution into seeking some kind of partnership if it needs expertise or facilities that are outside its own capacity.

Beyond that, it is possible to draw some general conclusions about the strengths and weaknesses of a range of technologies and the preconditions needed for their use. Some of these preconditions are about facilities needed by the teaching institution, such as access to broadcasting capacity for example, and others about what is needed by the learner. In looking at these options the planner will also need to consider where the costs are likely to fall and how they are shared between the teaching institution and the learner.

Technology choice is likely to be a function of access, cost and educational function. A technology is useful only if both the institution and the learner have appropriate access to it. The cost structure, and the possibility of economies of scale, differ from one technology to another. Plans also need to consider how far costs, in relation to any particular technology, fall on the tutor or the student. In making an educational choice the key distinction is between the use of technology to distribute teaching material and to allow two-way communication for tutor-student, and possibly student-student, interaction.

Paying for Government

Much, probably most, teacher education is paid for by governments. In particular, conventional full-time pre-service teacher education has generally been funded in this way with little if any cost falling on the student or on other sources of revenue. But this is not universally the case. Where teachers are enrolling individually, with institutions in the public or private sector, in order to get an extra qualification, they are often expected to meet some of the cost. And where teachers are studying part-time while they are employed, some governments argue that they can therefore meet some or all of the costs of their study themselves. The result is that distance-education programmes for teachers are funded from four different kinds of source: from government, from student fees, from the private, local and nongovernment sector, and from donors and funding agencies. Often a programme is funded from more than one source.

Funding agencies have long been responsible for some expenditure on teacher education, through government programmes as in Mongolia or nongovernment as with OLSET in South Africa. Generally, students are more likely to be asked to pay their own costs when they are enrolled as individuals, on a course leading to an advanced qualification. There are trade-offs between each of the options. If teacher education is seen as fundamental to the quality of education, then there is a public-policy argument for its being funded directly by a ministry of education, alongside primary and secondary education.

In practice, the shortage of central government funds have led some institutions to seek funds outside the ministry or to pass on some of the costs to the learners. While this may bring flexibility for the manager, the imposition of student fees may hold down enrolment and is likely to discourage students and to be socially regressive. There is little reported experience of the use of community resources in teacher education of this kind. Nongovernment organisations have played a part in some countries. In Brazil, for example, funding was generated by an established consortium while in South Africa OLSET has drawn funds from international funding agencies. While nongovernment organisations may have a freedom to innovate, and a freedom from government regulation, these have to be balanced against difficulties they may face in integrating their work with regular state activity and in achieving long-term sustainability.

External finance from funding agencies in particular may be unsustainable. Many funding agencies have been willing to meet capital costs, and to fund pilot projects, but expect governments to meet recurrent and continuing costs. The trade-off here is often between initial freedom of action, bought with external funds, and long-term integration and sustainability. If a teacher-education programme is more than a one-off solution to a crisis, then those questions of sustainability need attention from the outset.

The planner needs to consider trade-offs between alternative sources of funding which may include government funds, student fees, the private, local and nongovernment sector, and funding agencies. In considering these trade-offs, questions of equity and access and of sustainability, are likely to be all-important.

Accreditation and Assessment

Accreditation and assessment are linked and sometimes present particular difficulties for distance education. Accreditation refers to formal recognition of learning while assessment may relate to any process of testing students. In principle, giving credit for teacher education at a distance is no different from its award for conventional programmes. In practice, difficulties of two kinds have been faced. The first set of difficulties is about parity of esteem. If a distance teaching programme leads to a different qualification from that awarded for conventional course, the latter will generally be regarded as of higher status. If the same qualification, with the same examining structure, is used for two courses that are taught differently, then the methods of assessment may not be appropriate for one audience or the other. The second set of difficulties are about the practicality of examining, and in particular of examining any practical work, where students are scattered.

The link between the two sets bears on public perception of a qualification gained through distance education. Where distance-education programmes are tightly integrated with teacher education generally, both kinds of difficulty are minimised. Where, for example, distance education is part of the normal pattern of teacher education, with all students doing some of this in college and some at a distance, then problems of examining and of acceptability are likely to be reduced.

2

Pedagogical Methods of Teacher Training

The pedagogical concepts in which teachers are indoctrinated shape the education community's preference for schooling that is relatively ineffective and inefficient. Teachers are taught that it is more important to use stimulating and engaging practices than to use effective ones.

Changing Educational Priorities

The differences between consumers and providers go beyond factors such as professional expertise and familiarity with schoolhouse life. They stem both from different concepts of education and from practical considerations. In a word, both consumers and educators want the best for children, but they have different ideas about what is important. Consumers want results. Educators agree, but they believe that policy makers should defer to the education community's judgment in defining the result and setting the process by which it is measured.

Public education's consumers believe that schools should teach children the knowledge and skills that parents and taxpayers consider essential for happy, responsible, and productive lives. Through their elected representatives, the public establishes curricula; states course and grade-level objectives; sets policies regarding report cards, standardised tests, and so on; and otherwise acts to ensure that students will learn that which their parents and other members of the community expect them to learn. Education's consumers believe that effective schools and effective teachers are those that are successful in bringing about prescribed results and that true educational reform should serve to improve these results.

Teachers, professors of education, educators who work for the state education agencies, and other members of the education community, that is, public education's providers, generally take a different view. They believe that the knowledge and skills that consumers consider important are only one part of a broad range of considerations with which schools and teachers must concern themselves. They value academic achievement, but not necessarily as a top priority.

They believe that children have varied needs and that ideally schooling should be accommodated to those differences in a way that optimises overall educational growth-they are concerned with the "whole child." Education's providers hold as ideal those teaching methodologies that are intended to guide or encourage or facilitate "educational growth" in ways that are sensitive to student differences.

They denigrate and oppose the use of those methods that prescribe, expect, or require unaccustomed levels of student effort and accomplishment. They favour flexible curricula, narrative report cards, portfolio assessment, and teacher autonomy. They resist prescriptive curricula, letter grades, standardised tests, and teacher accountability. They believe that good schools and good teachers are those that maximise stimulation and opportunities for student enrichment, and they think of educational improvement as growth in the availability of enriching educational experiences.

Both education's consumers and education's providers talk about learning and achievement, but they accord it very different priorities. Educators believe that using correct pedagogical process is more important than attaining any particular level of mastery. Their reason for valuing process over outcome is that they believe optimal educational outcomes-that is, a kind of balanced growth of the whole-are possible only when the right kind of teaching is used. They refer to such teaching as "best practice." Best practice teaching is the open-ended, facilitative, guide on-the-side type of teaching that is extolled by professors of education.

It is also called learner-centered instruction because it theoretically puts the overall interests of the learner first-in other words, ahead of the teacher's interest in the student's acquisition of knowledge and skills. In the world of teacher education, learner-centered instruction is the standard against which all other forms of teaching are judged. In theory, learner-centered instruction permits the student to grow in a way that respects the full range of individual needs, not simply in ways that parents or teachers believe important.

Instruction fitted to individual student needs is believed to be conducive to the emergence of a personal synthesis of understanding, that is, an understanding that is practical, not abstract and bookish, relevant to the learner's life, and fully integrated into the individual's worldview. For example, in constructivism-a popular learner-centered view-the desired outcome of an educational experience is for the learner to construct personal meaning.

Learner-centered instruction is intended to be naturalistic-the sort of learning that takes place when experience is the teacher. When experience teaches, however, one never knows whether that which was taught is that which was learned; and to education's consumers, uncertain outcomes are a problem. They believe that certain types of knowledge and skills must be attained for an individual to become a productive and responsible member of society. They also believe that schools should urge students to maximise their talents.

These are subtle but enormously significant differences. Learner-centered instruction is not simply an alternative means of arriving at the objectives sought by parents and policy makers. It is an approach that places a distinctly lower value on students knowing and understanding the accumulated wisdom of past generations. Instead, it emphasises individuals forming their own ideas and assessing the worth of these insights from their immediate life experiences, that is, from the school of hard knocks. It is an approach that claims to equip students with thinking skills instead of knowledge. The public, by contrast, disagrees that thinking skills are sufficient even if it were possible to produce them in isolation.

Kids might find the unstructured approach more fun and might consider the organised lessons boring, but few parents would be willing to pay for discovery-based golf or tennis instruction-and neither would taxpayers. Yet that is the ideal taught to most teachers. More to the point, boring or not, starting with the basics is a far more certain means of producing skilled golfers and tennis players, and, plainly, that is the premier consideration with regard to basic skills like reading, writing, and arithmetic.

Kids can live without golf or tennis skills, but they can't do without sound academics. That's why parents want teachers to teach rather than just facilitate and hope for the best. Responsible adults understand what school success or failure means to a child's future, so they want children to learn certain things and they want those things learned to the best of the child's ability. Schooling is valuable precisely because it equips children with knowledge and skills that they do not yet recognise as important.

Pedagogical Doctrine in School Effectiveness

As a practical matter, educators recognise that not all students respond well to learner-centered instruction, and they have an explanation: not all students are "ready to learn." They believe students fail to respond properly because their life circumstances have not adequately prepared them and/or because there is some mismatch between the student's unique characteristics and the opportunities afforded by the school. In principle, at least, if society can give proper support and if schools can respond properly to their unique characteristics, the talents, interests, and energies of each student will be freed for intellectual pursuits. In other words, "all students can learn," that is, all students can benefit from "best practice" teaching.

Although described in a variety of ways, this concept of teaching's relationship to learning has been a staple of mainstream pedagogy since the early years of the twentieth century. It was the foundation of the child-centered teaching of the twenties and the progressive education of the thirties and forties. In theory, teachers trained in "enlightened" classroom methods would be helpful and sympathetic mentors, not taskmasters with a hickory stick. It was a concept that greatly bolstered public acceptance of the idea that teachers need specialised training, not mere subject matter expertise. It began as the "learning can be fun" approach, and it has become the "learning must be fun" approach.

Diversity of Fitting Instruction

Over the last thirty or forty years, learner-centered methods have attempted to individualise instruction to a variety of cognitive, developmental, socioeconomic, cultural, racial, and personality characteristics. The study of student diversity has become the overweening passion of education professors; and teachers, of course, have been thoroughly indoctrinated with the idea that their first responsibility is to be aware of and sensitive to such differences in their curricular and instructional planning.

There are mountains of research on the identification of student differences and an equally large number of studies showing degrees of relationship between student characteristics and success in school. However, what is lacking in most cases is any convincing evidence that teachers can fine-tune instruction to these differences in such a way as to produce significant improvements in measured achievement. In fact, the entire vein of educational research called "attribute treatment interaction studies" is generally conceded to have been a failure. What teachers are told, however, is that student differences are important and that if their teaching is truly creative, energetic, and engaging, they will succeed in individualising and bringing forth the best from all students.

In effect, teachers are being taught to make diagnoses that heighten their awareness of differences without advancing their ability to teach. Attention to diversity may not have made teachers more effective, but it has influenced their ideas about how schooling should be improved. If individualisation is necessary to learning, lower pupil-teacher ratios and the use of specialised personnel are the key prerequisites to any real improvement.

Conceptually, more personnel permit greater differentiation of services and therefore a better fit for each student. Educators say to parents: "Does your child have different developmental needs? Then he or she needs a teacher specially trained to work with those needs." "Your child has different talents? Then your child needs a teacher trained to maximise those talents." "Your child is racially or culturally different? Then your child needs a teacher who can fit his or her teaching to those differences." One impact of this thinking as it has been applied over the last century has been an incredible expansion and diversification of school staffing. If there is an identifiable uniqueness (and a supportive constituency), the education community will create a speciality that is said to be skilled in maximising the educational growth of such students.

School personnel now include not only a variety of subject matter specialists but also teachers trained specifically for middle schools, primary schools, kindergartens, and preschools. In addition, there are arts, music, and physical education teachers as well as trained counsellors, psychologists, nurses, social workers, and a huge variety of special educators, all overseen by layer upon layer of supervisory and administrative personnel.

Cost Effectiveness

As Eric Hanushek points out, the academic gains garnered by adding personnel and lowering class size have been small and costly relative to other means of increasing achievement. For example, far greater gains are attainable-and at much lower cost-using proven, result-oriented teaching methods. However, educators rarely adopt result-oriented methods, much less experimentally proven methods because virtually all such methods disagree with the learner-centered, wholechild, balanced-outcomes ideals promulgated by the schools of education. Instead of seeking to accommodate to student differences, result-oriented methods seek first to bring about learning. If accommodating to a particular uniqueness-entry-level knowledge and skill, for example-is known to produce improvement in learning, result-oriented methods acknowledge and make use of them. Otherwise, they ignore them.

Teachers are taught that any methodology that ignores learner-centered ideals is, in effect, a step toward the return of the hickory stick. They are given to believe that any deviation from methodology intended to address the growth of the "whole child" is a risky scheme. Of course, such claims are founded on belief, not research, but they have a profound impact on the kind of practices teachers favour and the kind they avoid. Instead of looking for the most stimulating and engaging methods among those that are known to be effective, teachers are taught to do the reverse. They look among the fun methods and try to find ones that produce results. The outcome, of course, is the sort of "edutainment" that is commonly found in today's public school classrooms.

A prime example of an effective teaching methodology rejected on the grounds that it conflicts with pedagogical doctrine is Direct Instruction (DI), which is a highly structured approach with scripted lesson plans. DI is as thoroughly tested and proven a teaching methodology as has ever been developed, and it has been around for thirty years. In Project Follow Through-one of the largest educational experiments ever conducted-not only was Direct Instruction the most effective, but it also did the best job of boosting student self-esteem, the personal growth that teacher educators claim will be undermined by an overemphasis on achievement.

Teachers, nonetheless, have ignored and rejected DI because it deviates from the learner-centered ideal. Despite an absence of credible negative evidence, they suspect that it has an adverse effect on student and teacher creativity. In matters of pedagogical effectiveness, evidence has little impact because teachers are inundated with learner-centered propaganda. For example, anyone reading the curricular guidelines of an organisation like the National Association for the Education of Young Children (NAEYC) would suppose that one of the greatest risks to the educational well-being of American children is academic burn-out resulting from premature attempts to teach the ABCs, teaching children before they were "developmentally ready." Of course, the opposite is true.

The greatest hazard to the educational well-being of American children is the failure of schools to teach them basics such as the ABCs. What the NAEYC and so many other educators fail to consider is that whatever the suspected risk from overzealous teaching, it must be balanced against the enormous and well-documented risk of failing to teach.

New Reforms in Teacher Education

Training in pedagogy that treats measured student achievement as an incidental outcome of some ideal form of pedagogical practice in which the teacher education community's notions about ideal process are considered more important than the consuming public's desire for improved student achievement. For decades, members of the lay public and lay policy makers have prodded, encouraged, and supported the education community's efforts at improvement. What they have gotten in return is a seemingly unending cycle of innovations, fads, failures, and reforms, most of which have been variants or refinements of pedagogical ideals that have been around since the early part of the last century. These "improvements" are coming right out of the schools of education, and they are creating problems, not merely failing to solve them.

Taxpayers are spending zillions on educational reforms that have been necessitated by the faulty and ineffective practices in which teachers have been trained. The self-esteem-boosting fad of the sixties and seventies is an excellent example. Proponents believed that students fail to benefit from schooling because they lack positive self-regard. In many schools of education, teachers were taught that the student's need for self-esteem must be fulfilled before study, learning, and achievement can be expected. Whole courses were dedicated to teaching teachers how to facilitate the growth of self-esteem.

Self-esteem improvement became so thoroughly ingrained in teaching that, at one point, U.S. students may have been world leaders in self-esteem despite their abysmal academic performance. As is the case with class-size reduction, there was research showing a modest relationship between high levels of self-esteem and academic achievement. As it turns out, however, self-esteem was related to school success not because high self-esteem is necessary to learning but because academic success elevates self-esteem. In other words, the self-esteem researchers had it backward. Improved self-esteem is a by-product of educational success, not a cause of it.

One of the programmes tested in the above-noted Follow Through Project of the sixties and seventies-the Open Education model-employed self-esteem boosting as its principal intervention. The students taught by this method did significantly worse on both basic academic skills and cognitive skills as a result of their participation. Neither have costs of any other of the many, many ideas that schools of education have propagated without any credible evidence that they work.

NCTAF Initiative

Now let's look at the current efforts to improve teacher

training. Will they prevent the re-emergence of nonsense like self-esteem boosting? Will they ensure that teachers are able to recognise the value of teaching models such as Direct Instruction? Will they require pedagogical enthusiasms such as whole language to be proven before they are disseminated? They are reforms embodying the same pedagogical doctrines that have underpinned teacher training for at least the last fifty years. The principal efforts to reform teacher training are being led by the National Commission on Teaching and America's Future (NCTAF).

The NCTAF is aggressively urging policy makers at the state level to adopt the training standards set by the National Council for the Accreditation of Teacher Education (NCATE); the teacher licensure standards set by the Interstate New Teacher Assessment and Support Consortium (INTASC, a group working under the auspices of the Council of Chief State School Officers); and the advanced teacher certification standards set by the National Board of Professional Teaching Standards (NBPTS).

This entire initiative is premised on the idea that the chief problems affecting teacher quality are insufficient numbers of fully trained teachers, insufficient training for teachers, insufficient regulation, and inadequate standards. Instead of training teachers to improve student achievement, current teacher-training programmes-including those that are NCATE-approved-are indoctrinating them in pedagogical concepts that embody educational priorities at odds with those of the consuming and taxpaying public. Adoption of the NCTAF proposals may improve teacher quality as conceived by the teacher education community, but if anything, it will make matters worse for education's consumers. Teachers not indoctrinated in learner-centered views will become harder to find.

The NCTAF is mainly composed of representatives of the education community. That they subscribe to the principles that have guided the education community for years is not surprising. The NCTAF has reams of research supporting its proposals, but virtually all are studies that define teacher quality in ways consistent with the education community's aims, not with those of the public. The NCTAF-inspired reforms are one more attempt to improve teacher training by promoting the wider use of pedagogical practices that have failed for generations.

They propose to look at both subject matter knowledge and pedagogical expertise. The concept of testing teachers for subject matter competence is sound because knowledge is a valid prerequisite to successful teaching and credible tests are available. As many have noted, teachers cannot teach what they don't know.

The assessment of pedagogical expertise, however, is another matter entirely. Policy makers and the public assume that tests such as the Praxis (formerly the National Teachers Examination) can measure a teacher's ability to bring about student achievement. In fact, they are not valid in that sense at all. Rather, they measure whether teachers have learned that which their professors taught them, which is the "best practices" favoured by the schools of education.

As was made clear by the recent report of the National Research Council's Committee on Assessment and Teacher Quality, "There is currently little evidence available about the extent to which widely used teacher licensure tests distinguish between candidates who are minimally competent to teach and those who are not." "[Teacher licensure tests] are not designed to predict who will become effective teachers." The same can be said about all of the various portfolios, rubrics, and classroom performance indicators that are embodied in the "competency-based" approaches to teacher assessment now recommended by the NCATE, the INTASC, and the NBPTS.

All afford the candidate the opportunity to exhibit his or her grasp of "pedagogically correct" methodology, not of practices that are known to bring about increases in measured achievement. From a consumer standpoint, these assessments are nothing more than a new way of ensuring that trained teachers are all grounded in the same ill-suited doctrines. Several recent reports agree that sound methods of assessing teacher quality are sorely needed.

A 1999 U.S. Department of Education report concluded, ". . . indicators of teacher preparation and qualifications do not directly address the actual quality of instructional practices." Similarly, an April 2000 report by the American Federation of Teachers called for teacher-training programmes to develop a credible core curriculum in pedagogy: "We can no longer tolerate a 'do your own thing' pedagogy curriculum." An improved exit/licensure test was one of its major recommendations.

A fall 1999 report by the American Council on Education not only called for improved assessment of teachers but also bluntly urged college presidents to either strengthen the quality of teacher-training programmes or close them. Tests of pedagogical knowledge and competency-based assessments of pedagogical skill are valid to the extent that they serve as proxies for effective teaching. In other words, they are valid to the extent that they predict what a teacher will actually do with students. The problem, however, is that the available tests and assessments have all been validated against the criterion of what teachers and professors think novice teachers should know and be able to do rather than what the public wants them to know and be able to do. In other words, buried in the debate about teacher quality are competing definitions of quality. One is quality as defined by the NCTAF et al., and the other is quality as defined by the public and by value-added assessment.

Teacher Effectiveness and Public

Value-added assessment of a novice teacher's ability to bring about student achievement solves the problems of uncertainty and bias in the assessment of teacher competence by observing the criterion of teacher effectiveness instead of its fallible predictors. It defines teacher quality as the demonstrated ability to increase student achievement, the public's definition. With value-added assessment, policy makers would no longer be dependent on test scores and subjective interpretations that embody a hidden set of educational priorities. Instead, they would, in effect, stipulate the meaning of teacher effectiveness and teacher-training effectiveness in a way that is aligned with the public's educational priorities.

Unlike training in law and medicine, teacher education has never had to respect consumer priorities because its graduates have never had to survive in a marketplace. Top-down regulation of teacher training has been largely ineffective, as well. The agencies in charge of regulating teacher education were originally formed to promote the expansion and enhancement of public education, not to perform oversight and control. They have been subject to what economists call "regulatory capture"-they are unduly influenced by the parties they are trying to regulate. The training, licensure, and certification standards now in place were all approved by state education agencies.

With value-added indicators of teacher effectiveness in place, policy makers would be able to identify successful programmes and adjust their support accordingly. School officials would have a much improved basis for making hiring, tenure, and promotion decisions, and parents, of course, would be pleased to have assurance that their child's teachers were meeting objectively measured performance standards.

Teachers, perhaps more than anyone, would benefit from a change to objective assessment of their work. One of the most frustrating aspects of teaching is that you can do an excellent job of getting students to learn and your efforts may never be noticed, much less appreciated. Even if test scores are reviewed, they are subject to administrator interpretation; and teachers well understand that friendly administrators make friendly interpretations and unfriendly administrators make unfriendly ones. With value-added assessment, the results are visible and they speak for themselves.

Subjective job performance assessments flavoured with favouritism are among the most demoralising and demeaning aspects of teaching in public education. In the absence of objective performance data, it is no wonder that teachers prefer salary schedules based on time-in-grade and earned credentials. The value-added assessments of teacher performance have been in place for some years, teachers are gradually being won over. Students seeking a career in teaching would also be able to make good use of value-added data. They would be able to see which schools of education were training effective teachers and which school systems were hiring them. Over time, teacher-training programmes whose graduates get the good jobs would flourish and those whose graduates were less successful would decline.

Title II of the 1998 Higher Education Act required teacher-training programmes to report on the quality of their graduates. One problem has been a lack of data comparable from one state to another. Realistically, programme assessments based on the value-added performance of novice teachers would have to be phased in over a period of several years. Substantial rethinking and curricular adjustment would be necessary. The change would not be easy, if for no other reason than shortages in appropriately trained faculty. However, with the growth of on-site training in local schools and similar alternatives, the need for trained teachers would be served by either reformed schools of education or their replacements.

3

Technology and Skills in Emerging Educational Environment

Family involvement teacher training was often traditional in definition, teaching methods, and delivery. Table 1 lists types and methods of pre-service family involvement training. It also notes where in the curriculum such training was offered. The vast majority of courses addressing family involvement dealt with parent-teacher conferences and parents as teachers. Family involvement was most frequently addressed in discussion and in required readings. Also, family involvement training was most often offered as part of a required course and in student teaching. Fewer than half of the programmes provided a full course on family involvement.

Table 1. Content of Family Involvement Curriculum in Teacher Education Programmes (n=60)

Types Addressed in Courses	%	Teaching Methods	%
Parent-teacher conferences	88	Discussion	92
Parent teaching child at home	80	Required reading	90
Parent as class volunteer	67	Lecture	86

Parent as school decision maker	63	Class assignments	73
Open house events	43	Case method	56
General family involvement*	34	Video/multimedia	55
Communicating with parents*	23	Optional reading	44
Understanding parents/families*	21	Direct work with parents*	23
		Guest speakers*	21
		Role play*	10

* "other" responses

Where in Curriculum Family Involvement is Taught	%
Part of a required course	83
Student teaching	63
Full required course	37
Field placement	36
Optional course	30
Seminar	25

Teacher education programmes, like state certification, lack a comprehensive definition of family involvement. The programmes still emphasize the traditional parent-teacher conference over contemporary family involvement activities. Although parent-teacher conferences are important, schools and teachers must recognize that families often need additional assistance and encouragement to help their children in school. This assistance ranges from providing parents with ways to help their children with particular homework assignments, to offering basic parenting education classes and more extensive family support services.

Evidence suggests that such assistance may be essential for many minority and low-income parents, in particular, for whom school involvement is often an intimidating and difficult proposition. In order for this type of family involvement to take place, however, teachers and schools must recognize the intrinsic worth of families as contributors to children's learning, and be willing to go beyond the traditional roles of parents and schools.

CERTIFICATION AND TRAINING

Most family involvement language in state certification requirements occurred in early childhood certification. Likewise, among the teacher education programmes surveyed, more family involvement training existed at the early childhood level than at all other levels. Early childhood programmes had more full required courses addressing family involvement, offered more hours of family involvement training, used "guest speakers" for teaching family involvement more frequently, and had more courses addressing an "understanding of parents" than did K-12 programmes.

The quality of family involvement training also appeared to be higher at the early childhood level than at the K-12 levels. Family involvement was integrated into the curriculum of early childhood programmes, where it appeared in a variety of courses and field experiences. In addition, innovative methods for teaching family involvement existed in early childhood programmes. For example, one early childhood teacher education programme had a community service programme in which student volunteers provided tutoring, respite care, and child care, and learned how to work directly with families.

Pre-service Family Involvement Training

Most teacher education programmes planned to incorporate

training in family involvement (Table 2). Almost two-thirds of respondents from the teacher education survey planned to increase attention to this area. When asked why they intended to increase family involvement training, respondents suggested that students, teachers, parents, and the broader community would benefit from increased family involvement in schools. This finding shows that a positive attitude toward family involvement existed, and that Pre-service education was regarded as important in increasing family involvement: only one programme considered Pre-service education to be ineffective for teaching about family involvement.

Furthermore, respondents seemed particularly sensitive to individual and local needs, citing pressure from individuals, schools, and personnel as motivating forces for increasing family involvement training. When asked why they planned not to increase family involvement training, on the other hand, other programmes often cited the absence of pressure from external groups, such as professional organizations. Some also faulted state departments of education for requiring too much of the curriculum, while restricting the maximum number of course units allowed.

Within teacher education programmes, questions must be answered about where family involvement training should be delivered. At present, family involvement is addressed most often as part of a course or in student teaching. Which locations or combinations of locations are most effective for delivering Pre-service training? Research suggests that family involvement in schools is most effective when it occurs over an extended period and is pursued through several different activities.

Table 2. Plans for Making Changes in Family Involvement Training

Reasons for Not Increasing (n=19*)	%	Reasons for Increasing (n=36*)	%
No external pressure	47	Intrinsic value	47
Limited number of courses	42	For students, teachers, parents	47
Satisfaction with current level	26	For society In general	22
Lack of funding	16	Extrinsic forces	
Faculty unfamiliarity	5	Pressure from individuals	42
Lack of collaboration between areas	5	External pressure (e.g., mandates)	28
Newness of the movement	5		
Pre-service training ineffective	5	Restructuring	
		Curriculum	25
		Philosophy, mission	22
		Specific programme	19
		Research	6
		Multiculturalism	6
		Early childhood spillover	6

*Of 60 programmes surveyed, 36 planned to increase family involvement training, 19 had no plans to increase, and 5 did not respond.

Challenges of Teacher Education Programmes

In addition to the survey of 60 teacher education programmes, the research collected in-depth information on nine programmes with substantial offerings in family involvement training. Teacher educators from these programmes described the challenges to preparing teachers in family involvement at the Pre-service level: lack of a national technical assistance network to support model development and information dissemination; restrictive university and/or government policies; limited scale and resources of programmes; and resistant attitudes from key actors. Two of the challenges — restrictive policies and limited funding — reinforced the findings of the survey data on barriers to increasing family involvement training (Table 2).

Lack of A National Technical Assistance Network

Research revealed that no system existed to support research and model development for family involvement training at the pre-service level, to act as a clearinghouse of information, or to provide technical assistance. Teacher educators pointed to a lack of successful models to follow and learn from; an absence of research on the most promising strategies for preparing teachers in this domain; and a shortage of teacher education faculty, cooperating teachers, and school administrators with the required expertise for and commitment to preparing teachers in family involvement.

This absence of models often required teacher education programmes to "reinvent the wheel" when designing their curriculum. Several programmes felt that it was difficult to know where to start or how to teach about family involvement in a meaningful way. Likewise, some programmes might have been able to avoid difficulties that arose with supervision, debriefing, and evaluation had they known the experiences of other programmes. Universities also had difficulty locating schools, administrators, and cooperating teachers who could model effective home/school/community partnerships.

Restrictive Government Policies

State and federal mandates, as well as universities

themselves, place many restrictions and requirements on teacher education programmes. For example, research revealed that states limited the number of education credits that could be earned, imposed academic majors on education students, and mandated various other requirements. Teacher education programmes were often required to include many topics within a limited number of courses, posing a considerable challenge to programme restructuring and the integration of family involvement into the curriculum.

Limited Scale and Resources

Teacher education programmes often lack the human and financial resources to implement comprehensive training in family involvement. The research showed that faculty members' numerous responsibilities often limited the amount of time they could devote to a focus on family involvement. This lack of time was particularly noted when only one or two faculty members were responsible for teaching, supervising, and coordinating their programmes. These factors suggest that a strong number of faculty is needed to sustain a family involvement training programme.

Collaborations, such as those among faculty for curriculum development or those among university, school, and human service personnel to arrange field experiences, can be labour intensive and time consuming. Programmes also faced limited funding, especially when implementing field-based instruction that required participation from school teachers. "All we can do is say 'thank you'," one faculty member said of the inability to offer stipends to teacher instructors. External funding from federal or private grants supplemented a few programmes, but such funding is often scarce and competitive. Extra money was needed to provide stipends for cooperating school teachers, who can be difficult to recruit and retain if no compensation is available.

Resistant Attitudes

The negative attitudes frequently held by faculty members, cooperating teachers, school administrators, and pre-service teachers were also cited as barriers to preparing teachers in family involvement. Some respondents reported that, at times, schools had "blaming" attitudes toward families or a "We're the experts" approach to family involvement. Some faculty members resisted addressing family involvement because they placed a higher priority on teaching core academic subjects.

Newer Concepts of Learning Improvement

Over the past 50 years, the nature of family involvement has evolved from a narrowly defined concept into a much broader set of ideas. The traditional view of "parent involvement" includes activities that often are unidirectional (parents give something to the school); exclusive (only a small, "privileged" group of parents participate); and narrow in focus (centering mainly on children's achievement). Newer concepts focus on developing mutual partnerships, involving all families, and recognizing a range of types of family involvement.

This is reflected in the change from "parent involvement" to "family involvement," the latter indicating that all family members, including the extended family, contribute to children's learning and school improvement. Also, families — as contexts of human development — and not just children, deserve support and participation in educational matters. These changes imply that teacher preparation must reflect a more inclusive and comprehensive understanding of family involvement than it did in the past.

While other typologies of family involvement have been created, they consist of actual types of family involvement activities carried out in schools. The framework, illustrated in Table 3, differs from such typologies in its focus on the attitudes, skills, and knowledge that teachers need to work effectively with parents. For example, "General Family Knowledge," in this framework, is not a type of family involvement per se, but an area of *knowledge* that teachers need in order to work with parents.

Table 3.
Family Involvement Framework for Teacher Training

Type	Goals
General Family Involvement	To provide general information on the goals of, benefits of, and barriers to family involvement. To promote knowledge of, skills in, and positive attitudes toward involving parents.
General Family Knowledge	To promote knowledge of different families' cultural beliefs, childrearing practices, structures, and living environments. To promote an awareness of and respect for different backgrounds and lifestyles.
Home-School Communication	To provide various techniques and strategies to improve two-way communication between home and school (and/or parent and teacher).
Family Involvement in Learning Activities	To provide information on how to involve parents in their children's learning outside of the classroom.

Families Supporting Schools	To provide information on ways to involve parents in helping the school, both within and outside the classroom.
Schools Supporting Families	To examine how schools can support families' social, educational, and social service needs through parent education programmes, parent centers, and referrals to other community or social services.
Families as Change Agents	To introduce ways to support and involve parents and families in decision making, action research, child advocacy, parent and teacher training, and development of policy, programmes, and curriculum.

By providing a range of types of training, the framework overcomes the fragmentation in the way in which students learn about family involvement. Content knowledge is enhanced when presented in a progressive and integrated manner. The framework begins with general knowledge about family contributions to child development and school achievement, and then builds toward specialized knowledge such as ways in which schools can support families and families can support schools. These latter activities point to the need as well for new schools that enable teachers to practice their new skills.

Family involvement is more likely to occur when school policies encourage it and school administrators support and reward teachers for their efforts. The framework recognizes several approaches to training in family involvement, which can be used alone or in combination. Four major approaches illustrate the kinds of attitudes, knowledge, and skills that teachers can acquire to increase their effectiveness with families. The approaches include: (1) a functional approach that describes the roles and responsibilities of teachers and parents in promoting student achievement; (2) a parent empowerment approach based on the strengths of disenfranchised families; (3) a cultural competence approach that makes the school an inclusive, respectful setting where diversity is welcomed; and (4) a social capital approach that builds community support for education.

Table 3 identifies the different content areas and their goals. The nine programmes that illustrate the framework were chosen from the survey or were nominated by survey respondents. Therefore, these programmes may not represent the universe of exemplary programmes. However, each programme in this sample met three criteria: they commonly focused on family involvement as an important area for pre-service preparation; they engaged student teachers in hands-on activities; and they promoted a broad concept of family involvement that recognizes family strengths, the need for family support, and the importance of home-school collaboration. Notably, the programmes tended to demonstrate knowledge, skill development, and experiences in several content areas, as well as innovative methods of delivery.

Family involvement efforts are most successful when teachers and schools assume that all parents want to do their best for their children and can make important contributions to their children's education. Teachers need to understand the benefits of and barriers to family involvement. Teacher preparation can equip teachers with the knowledge and skills to encourage participation from parents, especially those who may seem difficult to involve.

By taking an approach that identifies and builds on family strengths and resources, teachers can build on the wealth of knowledge, experience, and skills that parents possess. Parents feel valued when teachers work in partnership with them. They gain confidence in their ability to contribute to their children's schooling, and as a result, they are more likely to become involved in their children's education.

In the early childhood programme, seven required courses have a family involvement component. An optional course, a required workshop, student teaching, and a field experience also have a family involvement component. Pre-service teachers attend guest lectures by parents who discuss issues related to parenting, finding appropriate child care, raising a child with special needs, and making the difficult transitions involved in sending a child to public school.

Faculty who teach courses in social work present lectures on family dynamics and related concerns, and a special educator talks about how Individual Family Service Plans are developed with families. Prospective teachers interview parents and other family members about issues pertinent to early childhood. They also interview their own families for an understanding of the ways in which their family experiences have influenced them as teachers. For example, when addressing the subject of social development, pre-service students consider their own social development: they examine the many influences in their lives that have contributed to their work with children and families.

General Family Knowledge

Understanding the many influences in the lives of children - both inside and outside the classroom - can enrich teacher efforts to develop a curriculum that is meaningful and relevant to student learning. Learning about the families of the children in their classrooms can also prepare teachers to enlist the participation of parents and other family members in encouraging and supervising their children's education. A number of factors can prevent teachers and family members from developing a strong working relationship, however. Increasingly, changing demographics have widened the gap between teachers' and families' economic, cultural, and linguistic backgrounds.

These gaps may strain or limit communication between teachers and parents. Economically disadvantaged and minority parents, in particular, face many obstacles to becoming involved in schools. These individuals frequently face language and literacy barriers, have no access to transportation to and from schools, have no experience in asking teachers and other school staff questions, and fear attending school events at night if they live in dangerous neighbourhoods. Teachers may have difficulty overcoming these obstacles or reaching out to parents who have backgrounds different from their own. Teacher preparation can provide knowledge and understanding of families and offer teachers learning experiences that bridge the worlds of home and school.

The Rural Special Education Project is a small, innovative programme whose goal is to prepare teachers to work with Navajo students with special needs, a very underserved population. The Rural Special Education Project is part of Northern Arizona University's (NAU) teacher education programme, which places approximately 800 student teachers in schools each year. Through the experience of cultural immersion, up to ten special education teachers participating in the Rural Special Education Project on the Navajo reservation in Kayenta, Arizona, learn to work with Navajo families and other members of Navajo communities.

Participants in the programme have many opportunities to learn about Navajo culture and language. They live on the reservation for the academic year and take courses on site with an NAU professor. Each of these pre-service teachers is also paired with a Navajo teacher aide who has been a student in the programme. These teacher aides are paid a stipend to help the NAU student teachers adapt to the community and learn about Navajo culture. Each month, the teacher aides bring participants to various cultural events and activities, such as a Navajo wedding, that involve the entire community. Participants must also attend all school board meetings, where they can observe community decision making in action.

Community field experiences are a key component of the Teachers for Diversity Programme, a graduate certification programme that prepares teachers to work successfully in diverse communities with elementary students whose backgrounds differ from their own. A subprogramme within the teacher education programme at the University Wisconsin at Madison, Teachers for Diversity admits approximately 25 graduate students each year to participate in the 15-month programme.

The programme is field-based and collaborates with four elementary schools that have diverse student populations. At least one-third of the faculty members in each of the schools must be willing to collaborate with the University. Before starting the programme, faculty meet with various segments of the community, including the superintendent and members of the teachers' unions and two community-based organizations — Centro Hispano and the South Madison Neighbourhood Center — to introduce themselves and explain what they hope to achieve.

At the beginning of their first semester, all students are placed in a community setting. Approximately seven students are placed together at the same site so that they are not isolated from one another. During the academic year, they are in the schools 15 hours each week, tutoring and/or leading small group or whole class activities. While working in the schools, these pre-service teachers also attend seminars given by University of Wisconsin faculty associates who spend several days a week on site. Pre-service teachers spend an additional five hours each week in a community setting.

In addition to attending the University seminars during the fall semester, the Pre-service teachers return to the University in the late afternoon or evening for additional classes. In the spring semester, they complete their full-time student teaching requirement at these schools. This nontraditional course sequence offers a unique opportunity for connecting direct experiences with educational theory.

Students in the programme learn about family involvement by working directly with community members whose children attend local schools. One assignment, for example, asks the Pre-service teachers to obtain information about a child's health and physical and social development from the child's family members and from community service providers familiar with the child. In this way, the programme promotes the idea that parents and other family members, as well as family professionals, are valuable resources to teachers and schools.

Table 4. Attitudes, Knowledge, and Skills for Teachers Based on Four Approaches

Functional Approach
Knowledge of different cultural beliefs, lifestyles, childrearing practices, family structures, and living environments

Attitude of respect for different backgrounds and lifestyles
Knowledge of the functions of families

Parent Empowerment
Attitude of support toward parents, focused on strengths rather than deficits
Knowledge of power differences among groups in society
Knowledge of the history of disenfranchised groups
Knowledge of the effects of a family's disadvantaged status on its interactions with teachers or other professionals
Knowledge of how families interact with schools and similar institutions
Cultural Competence
Knowledge about cultural influences on discipline, learning, and childrearing practices
Knowledge of personal assumptions, belief systems, and prejudices that can affect relationships with family and community
Skills in understanding and reversing negative stereotypes of parents, families, and community members
Social Capital
Knowledge that schools and homes have different norms and values, and that such differences influence partnerships between home and school
Knowledge of common values that span different cultures and institutions
Skills in conflict negotiation and consensus building

Home-School Communication

Effective communication between parents and teachers can strengthen parent involvement in a child's education. Through open and honest communication, parents and teachers begin to understand one another's ideas about learning, discipline, and other topics. Such communication helps parents and teachers to work together to improve an individual child's performance and to contribute to schoolwide policies which benefit all students in the school.

Teacher preparation can equip teachers with the skills to improve two-way communication between home and school.

Graduates who have taken the course have applied their new skills in the classroom in numerous ways. Some of them have scanned photos of themselves into letters to parents at the beginning of the school year to help personalize their introductions.

Role of Family Participation in Learning Activities

Teacher preparation can equip teachers with the skills to develop two-way learning between home and school. Teachers can promote family involvement in children's learning and development by acting as facilitators rather than experts. They can recommend activities that help parents promote their children's learning, including reading to their children, creating a physical setting conducive to study, and showing an interest in their children's schoolwork. Equally importantly, teachers can learn from parents — about childrearing practices and family skills and resources — and tailor suggestions for involvement activities to meet the individual circumstances of each family.

Since 1985, the Parent Power Project at California State University, Fresno, has been preparing teachers to work effectively, sensitively, and confidently with families, particularly families whose children have learning difficulties. This goal is achieved, in part, by matching pre-service teachers with families in the community. Pre-service and inservice teachers in regular and special education, as well as students in counselling and administration, enroll in a three-unit graduate-level course that fulfills a requirement for several credentials and professional licenses.

After an introduction to the course and a discussion of family issues, participants are matched with families with whom they carry out projects and activities for ten weeks. Activities include interviewing a family, reviewing school records with the family, conducting diagnostic teaching on the child, and modelling successful teaching strategies for family members. Participants must also write weekly progress reports and a final summary for the classroom teacher, lead a weekly parent discussion group and a children's self-esteem group, and compile a resource notebook with parents.

Beginning in the 13th week of the semester, participants expand on what they have learned during their work with the families. They complete school surveys and design family involvement programmes to implement in their current or future job situations. Many participants complete master's theses on some aspect of family involvement, which they then use to build programmes serving families. Master's students must disseminate the information from their theses at conferences, staff development institutes, faculty inservice programmes, and university classes.

Evaluation data collected from parents, teachers, and Parent Power teachers reveal improvement in grades and classroom behaviour as well as eased tensions at home because of involvement in the project. "It is very gratifying to watch my students grow to the point that they can make their own contribution to the field," says Deanna Evans-Schilling, programme founder and director. "There are numerous spin-off projects, and some students are entering doctoral programmes to pursue their interest in family involvement. Many say the course is the most useful one they have taken." In 1992, the Project was awarded the Christa McAuliffe Showcase Award for innovative curricula in teacher preparation programmes.

Families Supporting Schools

When parents and the community as a whole support schools, schools gain a vast network of resources. Parents and communities can cultivate the values and ethos to support education. According to James Coleman, private schools are more successful than public schools because they have higher levels of "social capital." Social capital consists of families' and schools' shared expectations and goals, which are reinforced through social interactions between children and adults. Communities high in social capital provide strong social networks and trusting relationships that give individuals access to a wide array of resources ranging from childrearing advice to assistance in times of crisis.

Preparing teachers to involve families in their children's schooling can help teachers to understand families, communicate with them, negotiate differences, and build consensus. This training enables teachers to participate in forums for parents, teachers, and other citizens to establish collective support for learning and student achievement. Teachers also develop the skills to involve parents and other family members as resources for the school.

Teachers have learned to conduct interviews under a wide range of circumstances, and to take advantage of every opportunity to investigate funds of knowledge, whether they are walking down the hall or are participating in a field trip. They also learn to focus on the strengths of the individuals whom they encounter through their work.

Schools support families by providing opportunities to strengthen parenting skills, enhance parent networks, and minimize the stresses of parenting. Increasingly, teachers deal with students and families challenged by poverty. Such stressful circumstances can inhibit effective parenting practices, and as a result, have negative effects on children's development and school achievement.

Although teachers should not be held responsible for meeting the needs of such families directly, they can learn to understand the connections between poverty, family functioning, and childrearing. They can be trained to work in "full-service schools" that are providing families additional support services such as health and mental health care, adult education, and social services.

The programme is dynamic and changes yearly, but always maintains a focus on the following: (1) the primary responsibility of schools to initiate contact with parents, who often regard school as a place where authority is never questioned; (2) teacher leadership; (3) parent education; and (4) multiple definitions of family involvement that range from getting children dressed and ready for school to PTA membership and representation for other parents.

Finally, pre- and post-test surveys over the first three years of this programme have revealed positive changes in the attitudes of parents, teachers, and children. In addition, informal talks with graduates of the programme reveal that they implement the skills learned in the programme and extend this knowledge even further. Some graduates have become home-school coordinators, and others have started their own programmes.

Families as Change Agents

Schools and teachers can promote informed decision

making among families by treating them with care and respect, and by offering them opportunities for critical reflection and participation. The range of decision making is broad and includes such diverse activities as promoting an individual child's learning, improving school facilities and programmes, and implementing school reform. Teachers can be prepared to support and involve parents and families in various types of decision making. Such preparation should focus on helping teachers to develop and understand the principles of an empowerment approach. It should also involve their acquiring skills in managing group dynamics, problem-solving, and conflict resolution.

The Urban Teacher Education Programme (UTEP) at Indiana University Northwest, in Gary, aims to improve urban education by increasing the number of minority teachers and the number of teachers who can successfully work in urban settings. The programme utilizes Professional Development Centers (PDCs) to educate both undergraduate and graduate students in three urban settings: an elementary school in Gary, a middle school in Hammond, and a high school in East Chicago.

PDCs involve a collaboration between universities and schools or parts of schools. Courses and field experiences are coordinated by professors and paid teacher instructors. Teacher instructors deliver seminars at the school and negotiate syllabi with professors teaching courses. One major concern addressed by UTEP is how teachers in urban settings can work effectively with urban parents, many of whom are reluctant to be involved in the life of the school. Traditionally, many urban parents have had negative experiences with teachers and schools, both as students and as parents.

Many have been contacted by schools only when their children are having problems, and consequently lack confidence or become defensive when relating to teachers. UTEP prepares teachers to overcome these barriers by building relationships with urban parents and involving them in the schools.

One unique aspect of UTEP is the involvement of parents in the design of the teacher education programme. For example, each PDC has a parent liaison. Also, a parent advisory board designs the community experience component of the programme, which includes a tour of major service agencies in the community. This community experience component has recently been integrated into existing courses. For example, students in the Psychology of Teaching course participate in a 21-hour placement in a community service agency, such as a library, urban league, or community center with a tutoring programme. Some students, in fact, choose to spend more time in their community placement than required.

The parent advisory board has also sponsored a school-based workshop entitled "Through the Eyes of the Child," which brought community professionals together with school staff, parents, and UTEP students. A doctor, social worker, school nurse, hospital representative, juvenile law enforcement agent, and DARE programme representative participated in the workshop, along with members of the religious community, parents, teachers, teacher aides, and counsellors.

Effective Methods for Teacher Preparation

No one method of instruction can prepare teachers to work effectively with families and communities. Instead, approaches must be comprehensive, integrated, and varied. Table 5 illustrates these teaching and learning methods in relation to the framework for teacher preparation in family involvement. The nine programmes shared common innovative practices. These practices focused on developing prospective teachers' problem-solving skills by exposing them to challenging situations which required them to negotiate sensitive issues.

The programmes also provided them with opportunities to work in schools and communities — often under the guidance of experienced professionals — where they were able to gain valuable communication and interpersonal skills, especially when dealing with families with very different backgrounds from their own. These community experiences also gave them the opportunity to develop collaborative skills with professionals from other disciplines. In addition, the programmes emphasized the application of research skills to develop a better understanding of families and communities. They encouraged the use of information about families to develop family involvement activities and to create supplemental materials for classroom use.

These programmes utilized guest speakers, role play, the case method, community experiences, research with families and communities, self-reflection, and interprofessional education.

Table 5. Teaching Methods

Type	Method
General Family Involvement	Guest speakers Research with families and communities Community experiences Self-reflection
General Family Knowledge	Case method Cultural immersion Community experiences

Home-School Communication	Research with families and communities
Family Involvement in Learning Activities	Community experiences Research with families and communities Self-reflection
Families Supporting Schools	Research with families and communities
Schools Supporting Families	Research with families and communities
Families as Change Agents	Interprofessional collaboration Community experiences

Guest Speakers

Attending guest lectures and discussions led by parents, practicing teachers, experts from other disciplines, or co-instructors in teacher education courses provides prospective teachers opportunities to learn from and interact with key players in children's education. Programme faculty and researchers alike attested to the benefits of drawing upon the expertise of parents, school personnel, and faculty in other disciplines to enrich teacher preparation.

Examples of guest speakers

— Programme graduates, who researched family involvement during their own teacher preparation programmes, talked about what they had learned from their projects and how they had applied that knowledge to their first weeks of teaching.

— A parent-school coordinator, parents with special needs children, social work faculty, and special educators described how Individual Family Service Plans are developed with families. A home-school coordinator spoke to prospective teachers about her work and discussed ways in which teachers could promote family involvement.

— A human development counselling specialist presented a parent effectiveness training model and discussed skills to use in parent-teacher conferences.

Role Play

Role play requires students to act out situations that they might face when working with parents. Role play gives prospective teachers simulated experience in communicating, handling difficult or threatening situations, and resolving conflict. By dramatizing situations, prospective teachers become emotionally engaged and learn in a "hands-on" manner about the situations that they will face in their classrooms. Because role play usually takes place in the university classroom, teacher educators can analyse their students' reactions and responses, and peers can give feedback. By alternately playing the roles of teacher and parent, prospective teachers can gain a better understanding of each perspective.

Examples of role play scenarios

— Negotiating differences of opinion with a parent

— Communicating with a parent about his or her child's poor performance or behaviour

— Conducting a parent-teacher conference

— Discussing a student portfolio with a parent

— Explaining a new curriculum to a parent

— Talking with a parent who is angry or upset

Case Method

In the case method, prospective teachers read about dilemmas or ambiguous situations that could arise in working with parents. After reading the cases, these students analyse and discuss them, referring to their own relevant experiences and to the theories and principles covered in class. Because the case method approach encourages prospective teachers to examine many possible responses to a particular situation, and to evaluate the merits and drawbacks of each of these responses, they are able to understand the complexities of home-school relationships. Students' analyses of these situations help them develop crucial problem-solving skills. The case method also offers students the opportunity to integrate their beliefs with known theories as they respond to complex and problematic, real-life situations.

Examples of the case method

— One programme used a case study example in which a young girl in a programme for migrant workers had difficulty being understood because she always held her hand over her mouth when she spoke. A month into the programme, the girl's teacher met the mother and discovered that she also spoke with her hand in front of her mouth, to hide the fact that she had no teeth. This case demonstrated that the child's communication problems were the result of her modelling her mother's behaviour. The class looked at this case from multiple perspectives. The goal was for students to avoid jumping to conclusions or making assumptions about children or families.

— Another programme presented a case in which a parent and teacher had different agendas for a parent-teacher conference. To analyse the case, students wrote a 15-page response to the parent, drawing from one of the developmental frameworks presented in class. Responses were read aloud to classmates acting in the role of the parent, who then gave feedback from that perspective.

Cultural Immersion

One way to learn about children from diverse ethnic backgrounds is to live as they do. Cultural immersion is especially helpful when the teaching force and student body come from different cultural and/or economic backgrounds.

Examples of cultural immersion

— In a former programme at Clark Atlanta University, prospective teachers, along with social work students, had the option of living in housing projects with the children and families whom they would one day serve.

— At Northern Arizona University, prospective teachers in special education can live and student teach on a Navajo reservation.

Community Experiences

During placement in community settings, such as human service agencies, children's homes, and community centers, prospective teachers can learn about services in the community and form relationships with family and community members in a non-school context. In programmes that prepare teachers to work in urban schools or in communities with linguistic and cultural diversity, community experiences tend to be emphasized. These experiences allow prospective teachers to see children in a variety of settings, become more visible in the community, and understand children's sociocultural contexts.

Examples of community experience

— At UTEP, the community experience component was designed by parents who were asked what they thought teachers should know about their children's community. The experience began with a tour of major service agencies in the community, including libraries, urban leagues, and community centers with educational components.

— Community experiences can also include helping families and communities. Working in a neighbourhood center, teaching ESL to parents, and providing weekend respite care for a family with a disabled child are some of the numerous ways in which prospective teachers are able to assist families and communities.

— The "Parent Buddy Project" arranges for prospective teachers to visit a family's home several times a semester. Sometimes "buddies" will offer to babysit so that parents can go to PTA meetings. In this way, the project not only helps prospective teachers learn about family life, it also helps parents become more involved with their children's education.

Research with Families and Communities

Research with families and communities can range from parent surveys to in-depth ethnographic interviews with families. This method offers teachers the opportunity to understand issues from the perspective of families and communities and to utilize their expertise and insight.

Teachers can learn from and interact with families of different cultural and economic backgrounds as they conduct their research. According to one programme respondent, this method sends the message: "I want to get to know you," rather than "I'm here to teach you something."

Examples of research projects with families and communities

Prospective teachers have:

— developed a parent questionnaire or entrance inventory after working with at least five parents of children with special needs and written a summary of findings

— interviewed their own parents about their respective childhood experiences

— interviewed families who had a child with special needs. The prospective teachers then reflected on what they had learned from the family and on the implications for working with children.

— conducted ethnographic interviews in children's homes to gather and document household knowledge. The information collected was then used to develop lesson plans.

— "shadowed" a child to gather information about the child's health, physical education, and social development and asked parents and family and community members for information

— produced a book of research abstracts based on the prospective teachers' research with parents.

Self-Reflection

Self-reflection techniques include journal writing and other assignments that ask teachers to think about their own family backgrounds, their assumptions about other families, and their attitudes toward working with families. The goal is for prospective teachers to consider how their own perspectives will influence their work with families, especially those very different from their own. Self-reflection can be combined with other methods used to teach family involvement. It helps teachers process what they are learning and make the experiences personally meaningful. Self-reflection is also useful for addressing cultural differences. Finally, this method helps prospective teachers uncover any negative feelings and assumptions that they might have which may inhibit them from building positive relationships between home and school.

Assignments for self-reflection

— When discussing social development, prospective teachers in one programme reflect on their own social development and on the ways in which their teachers influenced them. This introspection helps prospective teachers examine their own beliefs and learn how these beliefs might influence their future work with families.

— One faculty member teaches about issues of power in society (gender and minority status, for example) by asking students to analyse their own cultural perspectives (such as their cultural history, language, and literacy).

— In one programme, prospective teachers are asked to look at their own cultural experiences and history, think about the match between their family community culture and their school culture, and then discuss ways in which some children's home and school cultures differ.

Interprofessional Education

Interprofessional education is a new trend in preparing human service professionals. Schools of nursing, social work, and other disciplines join with schools of education to prepare teachers and other professionals working with children and families. The purpose of this strategy is to train a range of human service professionals to work more closely with one another, to work in an increasingly collaborative environment, and to deliver services more effectively to families by placing them at the center of the human service system.

Examples of interprofessional education

— One programme unites a school of education and an anthropology department to find new ways of working with families.

— Another programme brings teachers, administrators, and counsellors together in an intensive family involvement training experience.

Comprehensive interprofessional training programmes have the potential to prepare teachers and other human service professionals to work effectively with families. For example, teachers involved in such training programmes will be better prepared to identify children's and families' non-academic support needs and refer them to appropriate outside agencies and personnel. Promising models are currently being developed at Ohio State University, the University of Washington in Seattle, and Miami University in Ohio.

4

Technology Competencies

The Teacher Technology Competencies are a set of technology standards that define proficiency in using computer technology in the classroom. The competencies consist of computer-related skills grouped into four general domains:

1) Basic Technology Operation,

2) Personal and Professional Use of Technology Tools,

3) Social, Ethical, and Human Issues, and

4) Application of Technology in Instruction.

Each domain consists of a subset of specific skills; these are sequenced from simple to complex so that mastery of the skills is cumulative. Fundamental skills come first—like managing electronic files, using computerised databases and spreadsheets, sending and receiving e-mail messages, and creating documents with graphics.

These skills are prerequisites for more advanced skills, such as accessing online resources, creating desktop publishing documents, developing multimedia presentations, selecting and customising instructional software to fit students' needs, streamlining record-keeping and other administrative procedures with electronic tools, and observing the correct protocols in sharing intellectual property.

Computer Education for Teachers

Research tells that the single most important factor in determining the success of technology in the classroom is a teacher who is comfortable with and knowledgeable about computers. Yet many teachers, especially those who entered the teaching profession before technology assumed such a pervasive role in society, have had little or no special training in computers. Even teachers who can demonstrate basic computer literacy are unlikely to be familiar with the full range of tools that technology can offer, from spreadsheets to digital graphics to instructional software.

Kids already seem to get the hang of computers faster than adults. Won't they pick up computer skills on their own if they just have access to the right hardware and software? It's true that most children take to computers quickly because they've grown up in an electronic age. But being a wizard at playing computer games or cruising the Internet isn't the same as possessing the sophisticated technical skills that will be needed in the highly computerised workplace of the future.

To develop these skills, students must be able to use computers to collect data, solve problems, make decisions, share ideas, and manage and present information—all with an understanding of the real-world application of these activities. Such abilities are rarely intuitive; they must be fostered by teachers who appreciate the value of technology in the classroom and can provide guidance in using these tools productively.

TEACHERS NEED COMPETENCIES

Just as technology pervades all walks of life and almost every field of human endeavour, technology skills are becoming essential in all subject areas because the computer is now the universal vehicle for the acquisition and dissemination of information in all fields. What's more, technology belongs throughout the entire curriculum because of its extraordinary potential for enhancing learning. The learning process becomes active instead of passive because students control their own learning: they must think about and interact with what is on the computer screen.

Since computers can radically expand information access and communication, they especially benefit students with disabilities by increasing their participation in the learning process. Just as other professionals utilise specific technologies as tools to enhance their work, teachers must likewise become adept in putting technology to use as the field of educational software evolves with the various academic disciplines. Regardless of grade level or subject, technology can support teachers in numerous professional activities—first and foremost in stimulating learning in the classroom but also in simplifying their administrative duties, improving personal productivity, and advancing professional growth.

How do teachers acquire the knowledge and skills that are specified in the teacher technology competencies? Technology itself is an interactive medium for manipulating our world, so the process of acquiring the technology competencies must necessarily involve ample hands-on practice, access to a wide range of tools, and, most important, an opportunity to discover the impressive possibilities of technology.

Technology Integration and the Teacher Technology Competencies

Technology integration refers to the use of a wide range of technology tools across a broad spectrum of relevant and meaningful contexts. Although it must begin with fundamental computer skills, it includes any technology application that enhances creativity, decision making, problem solving, collaboration, and overall productivity in the learning process.

In a learning environment where technology is truly integrated and not an adjunct, students and teachers use technology tools to enhance all areas of the teaching and learning process. For example, with computers students can access, organise, and analyse a vast world of rich resources—whether downloading original source documents from the US Library of Congress or taking a virtual tour of a museum. Students on different campuses can collaborate on projects, sharing and accommodating their diverse perspectives. They can participate in original research projects that put them in touch with actual researchers in the field, and they can receive electronic mentoring from noted experts around the world.

Technology gives students powerful tools for communicating what they have learned, motivating them to learn more. Effectively managing a classroom where students engage in these activities in a manner that improves academic achievement requires a teacher with expertise in the sophisticated and increasingly complex field of instructional technology. The teacher technology competencies are designed to give teachers this expertise to select and use the technological resources that not only meet students' learning needs but also equip them with appropriate skills for the future.

Since technology changes so fast, won't these competencies be outdated in a year or two? In formulating this set of standards, the teacher technology competency committee has established a concurrent process for reviewing and validating the competencies. As the affiliated institutions incorporate the competencies into their respective training programmes, the Committee will periodically evaluate and refine specific elements of the competencies to ensure that they are not only congruent with the ever-changing shape of technology but also effective in achieving the desired training outcomes.

The modular design of the competencies makes it easy to revise the components and performance criteria within a domain to reflect technological advances in specific areas as well as students' learning needs. Periodic updating of the competencies, with corresponding adjustments in the teacher preparation and professional development programmes, will keep teachers abreast of the most recent developments in educational technology. Most important, the organic structure of the competencies and their action-based orientation will encourage teachers to make technology tools an integral part of all their professional activities.

Mastery of the Teacher Technology Competencies

Mastery of the Teacher Technology Competencies is demonstrated entirely by performance-based assessments. These involve satisfactory completion of a series of tasks that give evidence of proficiency in each skill. Teacher candidates are assessed in the first three domains; classroom teachers are assessed in all four domains, including technology integration.

The Teacher Technology Competencies are the outgrowth of a unique consortium of educators, all representing different perspectives but sharing a common goal: the wise use of community resources. Keeping up with the pace of technology isn't simply a matter of upgrading equipment and infrastructure; it also demands a parallel investment in human resources by continually upgrading the knowledge and skills of teachers as they apply the technology in the classroom. Since this issue confronts all types of school districts throughout the state, the competencies have wide applicability as a model.

These competencies are based on the ISTE (International Society for Technology in Education) National Standards and support the TEKS (Texas Essential Knowledge and Skills) for all content areas which require the integration of technology throughout the curriculum. The Teacher Technology Competencies Committee envisions these competencies as the building blocks of an exemplary system of educational technology that combines pedagogical integrity with real-world relevance, fostering a teaching and learning culture in which the computer is a tool as basic as the three R's.

In this culture, teachers will no longer have to struggle to adjust constantly to the rapidly changing technology environment. Rather, as part of a larger user community of professionals, teachers will possess the technical competence that enables them to enjoy the benefits of technology, understand its infinite potential, and look forward to new technological practices and products for improving the quality of students' learning experiences.

Technology Competencies Framework

Each of the following relates to Technology Competency

Framework Domains, descriptions of the Domains, and a list of Technology Topics which address the Domains. The pages following reflect the competencies related to each topic.

Domain 1: Basic Technology Operation

Instructional staff must be able to demonstrate the use of a multimedia computer system with related devices in order to run programmes; to access, generate, and manipulate data; and to communicate results.

1.1 Basic Operations

1.2 Technology Tools

Domain 2: Personal/Professional Use of Technology Tools

Instructional staff will apply tools for enhancing their own professional growth and productivity. They will use technology in communicating, collaborating, conducting research, and problem solving.

2.1 Word processing

2.2 Database

2.3 Spreadsheet

2.4 Graphics

2.5 Multimedia applications

2.6 Telecomputing

2.7 Teacher/administrative Applications

Domain 3: Social, Ethical, and Human Issues

Instructional staff will demonstrate knowledge of equity,

ethics, legal, and human issues concerning the use of computers and technology.

3.1 District guidelines—ethics / Acceptable Use Policy

Domain 4: Application of Technology in Instruction

Instructional staff will apply computers and related technologies to support instruction in their grade level and subject areas. They must plan and deliver instructional units that integrate a variety of software, applications, and learning tools. Lessons developed must reflect effective grouping and assessment strategies for diverse populations.

4.1 District vision

4.2 Classroom integration

5

Classroom Teacher Training Management

The Incredible Years Classroom Management Programme is a comprehensive video-tape and group discussion training programme that has demonstrated effectiveness for helping teachers assist students in their classrooms who have diagnosed conduct problems. The programme is also effective as a school-based prevention programme for use by teachers to promote social competence, particularly in those schools that serve children who are at socioeconomic disadvantage. The programme is offered to teachers in 4-6 fullday workshops by trainers who have been certified by the programme developer. The programme was designed with the broad goals of:

a) strengthening teacher's positive classroom management for managing misbehaviour, promoting positive relationships with difficult students, and strengthening social skills in the classroom, playground, and on the bus;

b) increasing home-school collaboration;

c) promoting child social competence and academic skills; and

d) decreasing child conduct problems in the classroom.

In addition, teachers learn to prevent peer rejection by helping aggressive children learn appropriate problem-solving strategies and helping their non-aggressive peers respond appropriately to aggression. Teachers also discuss the particular learning needs of children with biological deficits such as attention deficit hyperactivity disorder (e.g., heightened interest in novelty, need for concrete markers of success) so that they are sensitive to individual developmental differences and the relevance of these differences for enhanced teaching efforts that are positive, accepting, and consistent. Physical aggression in unstructured settings (e.g., playground and lunch room) is targeted for close monitoring, teaching and incentive programmes.

Rationale for Teacher Training

Recent studies have reported that 10 to 25% of preschool or early school age children meet the criteria for oppositional defiant disorder (ODD), meaning they display high rates of aggressive, disruptive, oppositional, hyperactive behaviour problems, and peer relationship difficulties. Once children with behaviour problems enter school, negative academic and social experiences contribute to the further development of conduct problems. Aggressive, disruptive children quickly become socially excluded by peers. This leads to fewer opportunities to interact socially and to learn appropriate friendship skills.

Over time, peers become mistrustful and respond to aggressive children in ways that increase the likelihood of reactive aggression. Evidence suggests that peer rejection eventually leads to association with deviant peers. Once children have formed deviant peer groups, the risk for continuing conduct disorders is even higher. Theories regarding the causes of child conduct problems include child biological and developmental risk factors; family risk factors; ineffective parenting; school risk factors; and peer and community risk factors.

Researchers have found that teacher behaviours and school characteristics such as low rates of teacher praise, little emphasis on individual responsibility and social competence, and high student-teacher ratio are linked to classroom aggression, delinquency, and poor academic performance. High-risk children are often clustered in classrooms with many other high-risk students, presenting teachers with additional management challenges. Rejecting and non-supportive responses from teachers further exacerbate the problems of aggressive children.

Such children often develop poor relationships with teachers and receive less support, nurturing, and teaching and more criticism in the classroom. Walker and Buckley reported that antisocial children were less likely to receive encouragement from teachers for appropriate behaviour and more likely to be punished for misbehavior than well-behaved children. Aggressive children are also frequently expelled from classrooms. The lack of teacher support and exclusion from the classroom leads to social and academic difficulties and contributes to the likelihood of future school dropout.

Recent research has shown that poorly managed classrooms have higher levels of classroom aggression and rejection that, in turn, influence the continuing escalation of individual child behaviour problems. A spiraling pattern of child negative behaviour and teacher reactivity can ultimately lead to parent demoralisation, withdrawal, and a lack of connection and consistency between the socialisation activities of the school and home. While most teachers want to be active partners in facilitating home-school involvement, many lack the confidence or training to work collaboratively with families. Unfortunately, teacher education programmes devote scan attention to training teachers in how to in build relationships with parents or in implementing social and emotional literacy curricula.

The negative cycle described above can be prevented when teachers develop nurturing relationships with students and their parents, establish clear classroom rules about bullying, prevent social isolation by peers, and offer a curriculum that includes emotional literacy, social skills, and conflict management. Considerable research has demonstrated that effective classroom management can reduce disruptive behaviour and enhance social and academic achievement . Well-trained teachers can help aggressive, disruptive, and uncooperative children to develop the appropriate social behaviour that is a prerequisite for success in school.

Teacher behaviours associated with improved classroom behaviour include the following: high levels of praise and social reinforcement; the use of proactive strategies such as preparing for transitions and establishing clear, predictable rules; using short, clear commands, warning, reminders, and distractions effectively; the use of tangible reinforcement systems for appropriate social behaviour; team-based rewards'; mild but consistent response costs for aggressive or disruptive behaviour; direct instruction in appropriate social and classroom behaviours, and problem-solving and self-management skills.

Research on the prevention of conduct disorders has been identified as one of the nation's highest priorities. This agenda is vitally important because the widespread occurrence of adolescent delinquency and violence result in a high cost to society. "Early onset" aggressive behaviour problems in preschool children are stable over time and appear to be the most important behavioural risk factor for antisocial behaviour in adolescence. Such behaviour in children under 12 years of age has repeatedly been found to predict the development of drug abuse in adolescence as well as other problems such as juvenile delinquency, depression, violent behaviour, and school dropout. Since conduct disorder becomes increasingly resistant to change over time, intervention that begins in the early school years is clearly a strategic way to prevent or reduce aggressive behaviour problems before they "ripple" to result in well-established negative reputations, academic failure, and escalating violence in adolescence.

Over the past 20 years a variety of family and school interventions have been developed to address child conduct problems. When parents are trained in effective child management, their children become more pro-social and have fewer behaviour problems. However, while parent programmes lead to positive change at home, there has not necessarily been a corresponding improvement in the children's school behaviour unless teachers have been involved in the interventions.

As a consequence, Webster-Stratton developed The Incredible Years Classroom Management Programme for teachers. Over the past 7 years she and her group at the University of Washington have trained hundred's of Head

Start, preschool, and early elementary school teachers in this programme. When teachers are taught to work with parents, use positive classroom management techniques, and actively promote emotional literacy and social competence, they help not only the children who are at risk, but all children in the classroom.

Content of The Programme

Widespread support for teaching involving parents in their children's learning grows out of convincing evidence suggesting that family involvement has positive effects on children's academic achievement, social competence, and school quality. When schools work together with families to support learning, children tend to succeed not just in school, but throughout life."

Realising that student's cultural backgrounds, economic conditions, and home environments can profoundly affect their adjustment to and performance in school, schools are finding that they can best serve the needs of their students by becoming more family-centered and more focused on student's emotional and social as well as their academic needs.

Some innovative schools are providing nonacademic services to children and their families such as: parent education classes, parent resource rooms, GED classes for parents, employment training workshops, and special curricula for children that focus on teaching social skills, problemsolving and anger management strategies. Schools such as these demonstrate that the relationships between home and school are beginning to change in fundamental ways.

Teacher-parent Partnership

The training programme begins by asking teachers to brainstorm together the ways that they work with the parents of their students. The ideal relationship between the teacher and parent is based on a collaborative partnership. Collaboration implies a reciprocal relationship that uses the teacher's and parents' knowledge, strengths, and perspectives equally. The teacher is more knowledgeable about teaching principles, curriculum, and the child's learning needs, while the parent is more knowledgeable about the child's temperament, likes and dislikes, and emotional needs. Accepting the notion of complementary expertise creates a relationship between parents and teachers that is mutually respectful and supportive. In this non-blaming and nonhierarchical model, the teacher promotes collaboration through reflection, summary of parent suggestions, reinforcement, support, acceptance, humour, optimism, encouragement of parent participation, and sharing of her own ideas.

Despite the evidence of the positive effects of family involvement on a student's academic performance, its potential is still largely ignored in many schools. Many teachers do not systematically encourage parent involvement, and parents do not always participate even when they are encouraged to do so. Teachers may feel too stressed by classroom demands to invest the time needed to involve parents, they may believe that parents are not interested in participating in their children's education, or they may lack the training needed to successfully collaborate with parents.

Parents may feel intimidated or mistrustful of teachers, feel they lack the knowledge to help educate their children, or may be so overwhelmed by life stress that they have little energy to be involved in their child's schooling. In this context, teachers need training in family involvement that emphasises more than traditional parent-teacher conferences. Schools must recognise the additional assistance and encouragement that families need in order to help their children in school. Evidence suggests that such assistance may be essential for many minority and economically disadvantaged parents, in particular, for whom school involvement is often an intimidating and difficult proposition.

Positive Home-school Bonds

The parent involvement efforts need to start even before school starts. The more parents know about what is going on at school, the more connected they will feel to the teacher and classroom. The training encourages teachers to reach out to families in a variety of ways. For example, they might send home a "welcome" greeting to all families describing their philosophy of discipline, their homework policy, how and when they can be reached, and an invitation to first parent meeting. Teachers can also begin to gather information about the parents and children by including an interest survey asking about children's favourite activities and family interests. Forming an early bond is particularly important for students with a history of problems in school.

Calling the parents of these children before school starts to establish positive communication, reassure parents, and establish initial plans to work positively with the child will help the child to make the transition to a new classroom. When school begins, weekly newsletters, invitations to join the class for lunch or activities, phone calls home about student's positive progress, and home visits will help to encourage parent collaboration with the teacher and school.

Once a positive relationship is established between teachers and parents, it is easier to address later problems and concerns that arise.

Learning Problems

Sometimes teachers try to avoid conflict or disagreement with parents by not talking with them about children's behaviour or learning problems. They may not want to worry the child's parents and may hope that, left alone, the child will out-grow the problem. The core of successful collaboration with families, however, involves contacting parents at the first sign that a child is having difficulty. By involving parents early in the planning, teachers may discover family circumstances that are contributing to a child's difficult behaviour or they may gain valuable insights from parents about how to manage a particular behaviour. At the very least, they will have included the parent in the problem-solving process before the situation has escalated into a serious problem.

One of the most common complaints among parents is that teachers wait too long before contacting them about a school problem. Teachers may lack the confidence or skills to talk effectively with parents about problem behaviour. The training programme encourages teachers to use the following important steps to establishing good communication about a child's school problems:

— Call parents and offer flexible meeting times

— Express a positive caring attitude about the problem

— Ask for parent input

— Avoid blaming parent for problem

— Deal with one issue at a time

— Describe how you have tried to deal with the problem

— Ask how parents deal with similar problems at home

— Agree on mutual goals

— Problem-solve solutions together

— Set a follow-up meeting to review progress

Positive Relationships with Students

This component of the training programme emphasises the importance of building trusting and warm teacher-student relationships. Trainers begin by asking teachers to brainstorm ways they can build positive with their students, particularly those students for whom they have developed negative feelings. Perhaps the most obvious reason for teachers to develop meaningful relationships with students is because a positive teacher-student relationship built on trust, understanding and caring will foster students' cooperation, motivation, and increase their learning and achievement at school.

Relationship-building between teachers and students is important for all students, but it is vital for those students who are most aggressive, noncompliant, shy, withdrawn, or depressed. In other words, the students who are hardest to reach are those who will benefit most from a positive relationship. It is important to help teachers persist at engaging the most difficult students. When faced with repeated defiance and noncompliance, it is easy to take children's negative behaviour personally or to blame the child for not trying. As with parent-teacher relationships, getting to know children should begin before the school year starts. An introductory phone call or personal letter to the child telling them something special about their classroom and finding out about their interests will help to establish an initial bond. The training programme suggests the following strategies to help teachers build relationships with children during the school year:

Show caring by:

— Giving a personal greeting to each student every morning
— Asking about their feelings
— Asking about their life outside of school
— Listening to student stories and problems
— Eating lunch with students
— Recognising birthdays
— Sending cards and positive messages home
— Finding out about student hobbies and special talents
— Making home visits
— Attend a special event (i.e., sports event or performance that student is involved in)
— Sharing something personal
— Spending time playing with students-at recess or during free classroom time
— Use descriptive commenting when children are playing
— Make all children feel valued for contribution to class regardless of their academic or social abilities

Show belief in students by:

— Identifying negative self-talk

— Promoting positive self-talk

— Communicating the belief they can succeed

— Creating ways to acknowledge new skills or positive behaviours

— Calling students to applaud their special efforts or accomplishments

— Calling student after a bad day to predict a more successful next day

— Helping every child in the classroom to appreciate other's special talents and needs

— Following children's lead, listening carefully to their ideas and being an "appreciate audience" at times

Show trust in students by:

— Inviting students to help with daily tasks and classroom responsibilities

— Offering curriculum choices

— Encouraging collaboration among students

— Encouraging students to help each other

— Sharing thoughts and feelings with students

Proactive Teaching

When students are disruptive or behave in ways that are counterproductive to learning, it is easy for teachers to automatically react emotionally. This understandable impatience and frustration in response to negative behaviour undermines the ability to think strategically about the most effective response the child's behaviour. Teachers can learn to anticipate the kinds of classroom conditions that are likely to produce disruptive or disengaged behaviours and take proactive steps to prevent them. Research has shown that proactive teachers structure the classroom environment and the school day in ways that make problem behaviours less likely to occur. They establish schedules, routines, consistent limit setting, and norms of behaviour that help students know what to expect. Following are a few of the many proactive strategies that teachers discuss in the classroom management training:

— Develop clear, positive classroom rules and discuss them with children ahead of time

— Have predictable schedules and routines for handling transitions

— Capture children's attention before giving instructions

— Place inattentive or distractible children close to the teacher.

— Strive for clear, specific, commands expressed in positive terms.

— Redirect disengaged children by using their name in a question, standing near them, changing activities, and using nonverbal signals.

— Use positive reminders about the behaviour expected rather than negative statements when children are exceeding the limits.

— Give frequent attention, praise, and encouragement to children who are engaged and following directions.

— Be creative in your use of redirecting strategies-avoid repeated commands. Instead, use nonverbal cues and engaging activities.

Promoting Social Competence

The quality of the teacher's attention emerges as one of the most important factors in helping students become motivated and successful learners. Consistent and meaningful encouragement and praise from a teacher nurtures and increases children's academic and social competence. Children who are praised are self-confident, have high self-esteem, and seem to internalise these early messages so as not to need them in the future. Yet, teachers give three to fifteen times as much attention to student misbehavior than to positive behaviour in their classrooms. Not surprisingly, this attention reinforces the misbehavior, leading to more classroom behaviour problems, particularly in the child who is starved for adult attention.

When teachers use their attention selectively to reinforce positive behaviour, they see a dramatic impact in the behaviour of targeted children as well as on the rest of the children in the classroom. Over time, giving more praise and positive attention to children for their progress can be beneficial for all the students in the classroom because these labelled descriptions of the expected academic and social behaviours act as a reminder of expected behaviour for the other children.

Using Incentives

When students have difficulty with a particular behaviour or area of learning, praise and attention may not be enough to motivate them. Learning to read, write and behave in socially appropriate ways are difficult processes for some children. At times, tangible rewards can provide extra incentives for children to tackle difficult learning area, or can sustain a child's motivation until a positive relationship has been developed with the teacher that will make praise and attention more motivating. Stickers or tokens, special rewards, and celebrations to give students concrete evidence of their progress.

When using incentive programmes to motivate students to learn something new, it is, of course, important to continue providing social approval as well. Social rewards should be used to reinforce the efforts children make to master a new skill or behaviour. Tangible rewards are usually used to reinforce the achievement of a specific goal. Based on social learning research regarding incentive systems, trainers and teachers discuss the most effective and practical approaches to making incentives work. Following are some tips for successful incentive programmes:

Some Do's and Don'ts Do

1. Clearly define the desired academic and social behaviours.
2. Identify small steps towards the goals.
3. Gradually increase the criteria for the reward.
4. Begin by choosing only one or two behaviours to work on.
5. Focus on positive behaviours.
6. Choose inexpensive rewards.
7. Offer rewards that can be earned on a daily basis.
8. Involve students in choosing the rewards.

9. Give the reward after the behaviour occurs (first/then).
10. Reward everyday achievements and successes.

Don't:

1. Be vague about the desired behaviours.
2. Make the steps too big for the child.
3. Make the steps too easy for the child.
4. Create complex programmes involving too many behaviours.
5. Focus on negative behaviours.
6. Offer expensive rewards, or rewards that cannot be furnished immediately.
7. Use rewards that take too long to earn.
8. Choose rewards that are not motivating to the child.
9. Offer rewards as bribes.
10. Be stingy with social rewards.

Managing Misbehavior

Even with the best proactive classroom management, misbehavior will still occur. A discipline plan that clearly spells out rules, expectations, and consequences if the rules are broken is fundamental to successful management of disruptive behaviours. In the Discipline Plan, consequences should be organised in a hierarchy from the least disruptive intervention to the most disruptive. By making sure that students are familiar with the Discipline Plan and understand the consequences, the proactive teacher ensures that students know exactly how the teacher will respond to misbehavior. The consistency of the teachers' follow through with this Discipline Plan increases children's sense of security.

Minor inappropriate or low-level attention seeking behaviours such as whining, teasing, arguing, eye rolling, pouting, calling out, and tantrums can often be eliminated if they are systematically ignored. Teachers who ignore inappropriate behaviour remove the payoff for continuing these behaviours. If teachers consistently ignore particular behaviours, students will eventually stop engaging in those behaviours. Moreover, if students receive praise and encouragement for the opposite pro-social behaviours, they will learn it is more beneficial to behave appropriately. Following are some important points to remember when using ignoring and redirecting to reduce problem behaviour.

Ignoring and redirecting

— Ignoring works best for low-level attention seeking behaviours (make sure they are ones you can ignore).

— Praise the opposite pro-social behaviours.

— Avoid eye contact and discussion while ignoring.

— Physically move away from your student.

— Be prepared for testing-remember misbehavior often gets worse before it gets better.

— Be consistent.

— Return your attention as soon as misbehavior stops.

— Combine distractions and redirection with ignoring.

— Limit the number of behaviours to systematically ignore.

— Teach other students to ignore minor misbehaviours.

— Encouraging self-monitoring when possible.

— Don't ignore withdrawn behaviour-use re-directions to engage student.

— Use nonverbal signals and picture cues for redirecting.

— Young children benefit from physical redirection at times.

— Positive reminders are particularly useful for impulsive or distractible students.

Natural and logical consequences

No matter how consistently teachers use ignoring, redirecting, and reminders, and no matter how consistently they reinforce appropriate behaviour, there are times when children will continue to misbehave. In these cases, their misbehavior needs a negative consequence. A negative consequence is something the child does not want, such as being last in line, losing recess, getting Time Out in the classroom, or missing a special activity. Consequences do not have to be severe to be effective. The key is consistency, not severity. Whenever possible, consequences should be presented as a choice the child has made. For example, "You didn't share those blocks when I asked. That means you've chosen to play in another area today." During the training, the trainer leads a discussion with the teachers of the various ways they have used consequences.

The student who displays physical aggression needs to experience a more serious consequence. The task for teachers is to use discipline that teaches students that violent behaviours will not be tolerated, establishes positive expectations for future appropriate behaviour, and conveys to students that they are valued despite their mistakes. Ideally this discipline plan should be a whole-school plan and not just an individual teacher classroom concern. All teachers have a role for caring for all students and schools have a commitment to supporting all teachers in managing students with difficult behaviour problems. Thus it is important that all school staff work together to manage difficult behaviours.

A Time Out or Calm Down strategy is reserved specifically for high intensity problems, such as aggression toward peers or teachers and destructive behaviour. It is also useful for highly noncompliant, oppositional or defiant children , since compliance is the cornerstone of a parent's or teacher's ability to socialise a child. Time Out is probably the most intrusive short-term consequence a teacher will employ for disruptive behaviour. It can occur in the classroom as a cool-off time or it can involve temporary removal from the classroom to another classroom or a specially designated area in the school. Time Out can backfire if the process has not been carefully thought through and if children have not been prepared ahead of time. Trainers assist teachers in planning for how and where they will use Time Out in their classrooms. The following points are important when implementing Time Out:

— Preparation ahead-plan a hierarchy of responses to misbehaviours and inform students of the plan

— Rehearse the Time Out procedures with the children prior to doing a real Time Out

— Be prepared for testing

— Monitor your own anger,in order to avoid exploding suddenly; give warnings

— Use a 5-minute Time Out with 2-minute silence at the end

— Carefully limit the number of behaviours for which Time Out is used

— Use Time Out consistently for selected misbehaviours

— Don't threaten Time Out unless you're prepared to follow through

— Ignore child while in Time Out

— Use nonviolent approaches such as loss of privileges as a back-up to Time Out

— Hold children responsible for messes or destruction in Time Out

— Support co-teachers' use of Time Out

— Be sure you are rewarding the expected positive behaviours.

— Expect repeated learning trials

— Use personal Time Out to relax and refuel

— Gain parental support for your discipline plan.

Repair and Rebuild

Children who are impulsive, oppositional, inattentive, and aggressive will need constant teacher monitoring or scaffolding. This means giving redirection, warnings, reminders, and consistent follow-through with consequences. However, one of the hardest and most important things for a teacher to do when teaching a disruptive student is to move beyond Time Out and discipline to repair and rebuild positive teacher-student and student-student relationships. This means not holding onto grudges and resentments after consequences have been implemented, welcoming students back as accepted and valued members of the class each day, and continuing to teach them more effective ways of problem-solving.

It means a philosophy of taking one day at a time, allowing the student a new learning opportunity or fresh start each day, and practicing forgiveness. So, instead of saying, "I hope today is not going to be like yesterday, because if you are....", the teacher encourages the child and predicts a successful day: "I'm glad to see you. Today is a chance to learn something new."

Self-Management

Difficult and aggressive students will initially need tight external management and consistent discipline in order to keep their behaviour under control. Indeed, research has indicated that teacher use of incentives, differential reinforcement, Time Out, and negative consequences results in decreased negative classroom behaviours and increased positive social skills. However, the eventual goal is to shift away from exclusive teacher management to increasing student self-management skills. This is necessary so that students can become less dependent on teachers to provide direction and incentive for their behaviour. Such interventions have the potential for producing more durable and generaliseable behaviour gains in situations outside the classroom.

One of the central features of many children with behaviour problems is the absence of self-management skills. Part of the reason for this is that such children often have distorted self-perceptions and sense of reality and make mal-adaptive self-statements. They have difficulty evaluating their own behaviour; at times having an inflated sense of their performance and, other times, being very negative about their abilities. They may misperceive other's intentions as hostile, when in fact, the person might have been trying to be helpful. Although the degree of self-management expected of students will vary with the age, developmental ability and temperament of the child, teachers can begin to foster some skills of self-direction even in preschool children and children with severe disabilities. These skills are seldom taught to students, especially those with behaviour problems.

Self-management interventions generally involve a variety of strategies related to changing or maintaining one's own behaviour. They include self-evaluation and selfreinforcement approaches. For example, teachers can invite children to reflect on how they did that day to get a sense of the accuracy of their self-perceptions and self-evaluation abilities. For children who have poor language skills or limited emotional vocabulary, a teacher might have a thermometer showing the range from calm to overexcited and ask the child to point to how active or on-task he thought he was during certain times of the day. This gives the teacher an opportunity to provide students with specific feedback on the accuracy of their self-perceptions or to help them remember times when they were successful. Similar thermometers might be used for students to evaluate their ability to control their anger or their level of classroom involvement. Often children with behaviour problems will focus on their mistakes; however, by reviewing the positive aspects of the child's day, the teacher can help the child to gain more positive attributions.

Self-management interventions also include self-monitoring approaches such as the "quiet hand up" or "blurt out sheet" that is placed on a students' desk so that she could record each time she remembered not to talk out in class. The teachers might also challenge students to meet a certain criteria to earn a chosen reward. This approach makes self-monitoring exciting and results in a high degree of student involvement. Similar programmes could be set up for self-monitoring other behaviours such as on-task or "working" behaviour, polite language, or work completion. Teaching children self-instruction such as the internalisation of self-statements is another self-management approach used to modify problem behaviour.

For example, a child with academic difficulties who is off-task a great deal may be thinking negative thoughts that perpetuate the problem. Teaching positive self-statements can result in improved on-task work. Finally, social problem-solving training, described next, was developed to help children learn the thinking and social skills involved in making good choices and assuming responsibility for their own behaviour.

Social-Emotional Curriculum

Young children often react to their problems in ineffective ways. Some cry, tantrum, and yell, others hit, bite, and become destructive, and still others tattle or lie to their parents or teachers. These responses do little to help children find satisfying solutions to their problems. In fact, they create new ones. But research shows that children use these inappropriate strategies either because they have not been taught more appropriate ways to problem-solve or because their inappropriate strategies have been reinforced inadvertently by parents or teachers or other children's responses. Children who are hyperactive, impulsive, inattentive and aggressive are more likely to have cognitive difficulties with social problem-solving.

These children perceive social situations in hostile terms, generate fewer pro-social ways of solving interpersonal conflict, and anticipate fewer consequences for aggression. There is evidence that children who employ appropriate problem-solving strategies play more constructively, are better liked by their peers and are more cooperative at home and school. Consequently teachers have a key role in teaching children who are aggressive and impulsive to think of more pro-social solutions to their problems and to evaluate which solutions are better choices and more likely to lead to positive consequences than others. In essence, these high-risk students are provided with strategies that correct the flaws in their decision making process and reduce their risk of peer relationship problems.

Teachers can incorporate specific problem-solving lessons into their curriculum, provide students with opportunities to practice these new skills in small group activities, and promote newly learned skills throughout the day.

Problem solving-steps

1. What is my problem? (Identify the problem in concrete terms)
2. What are some solutions? (Generate as many different solutions as possible)
3. What are the consequences? What happens next?
4. What is the best solution or choice? (Evaluate consequences in terms of safety, fairness and good feelings)
5. Am I using my plan? (Implementation)

6. How did I do? (Evaluating the outcome and reinforcing efforts)

Important tips for teaching problem solving

- Use games and puppets to present hypothetical problems for students to practice the problem-solving steps
- Help students clearly define the problem and to recognise the feelings involved
- For preschool children, focus on generating many solutions
- For elementary age students, focus on thinking through to the various consequences of different solutions
- Be positive, creative and humorous
- Help children anticipate what to do next when a solution doesn't work
- Model effective problem-solving yourself
- Focus on the process of learning how to think about conflict, rather than on "correct" answers
- All children (not just the high-risk children) should be included in the process

Emotional regulation

Before students can effectively problem-solve, they need to be able to recognise and regulate their own emotional responses. Teachers can play a critical role in helping children learn to manage their anger. During training sessions teachers discuss how to help students think differently about why an event occurred, recognise and talk about their own feelings, read feeling cues in others, and teach them to employ self-talk and relaxation strategies to keep themselves calm. Teachers also act as powerful models for students whenever they can remain calm and nonaggressive in response to the negative classroom behaviour. The following tips are important in helping children to understand feelings and regulate their own emotions:

— Acknowledge individual differences in student's ability to regulate emotions

— Use feeling talk in the classroom. Label both negative and positive teacher and student feelings.

— Use games to teach the feelings language and to promote understanding of differences in others' feelings

— Teach children positive self-talk strategies

— Teach the "Turtle Technique" for managing anger

— Have children practice anger management responses to hypothetical conflict situations.

— Elicit the support of parents in managing anger and teaching child to express their feelings

Friendship Skills: Few teachers need to be convinced that friendships are important for children. Through the successful formation of friendships, children learn social skills such as cooperation, sharing, and conflict management. Friendships also foster a child's sense of group belonging and begin to facilitate children's empathy skills. Research has shown that peer isolation or rejection are predictive of a variety of problems including depression, school drop out, and other psychiatric problems in adolescence and adulthood. The trainer leads a discussion about how to prevent peer rejection and ways to help the aggressive or socially withdrawn or isolated child. Teachers should include the following specific friendship skills in their classroom curriculum:

— How to initiate an interaction and enter a group
— How to play in a friendly way: sharing, making a suggestion, waiting, asking for permission, taking turns, helping, giving a compliment, agreeing with each other, asking for help, being polite
— How to follow directions
— How to talk with friends
— Empathy training
— Problem-solving/conflict resolution.

Methods of teaching these friendship skills

— Use discussions and role plays to teach group entry skills, play skills, and conversational skills
— Set up cooperative learning activities to help students practice friendship skills
— Praise and establish reward programmes for student with social difficulties
— Collaborate with parents to promote children's social skills at home Teacher Training Methods

Teacher and School Engagement

Engaging teachers and schools in the training process is a multi-pronged process. If the goal is to offer the training programme to an entire school or agency, we begin laying the ground-work for the training at least six months before the actual training begins. It is important to meet with school administrators, teachers, and parents to listen to their concerns for their school, classrooms, and children in general, or for particularly challenging students. Teachers, administrators, or parents may want to talk to others who have previously been involved in the training in order to hear first-hand how the training benefited their schools.

Logistical details also need to be worked out far in advance, and administrative support must be obtained for the teachers who will be involved. If training is held during the school day, school must be prepared to cover the cost of substitute teachers. If the training is held after school, teachers need support so that they can complete their regular school-related tasks.

Video-tape Modelling

The programme relies heavily on video-tape modelling as a therapeutic method. Trainers present 6 video-tape programmes composed of over 250 brief vignettes showing teachers and children of different sexes, ages, cultures, socioeconomic backgrounds, temperamental styles and developmental abilities. Teachers and children are shown in their classrooms in unrehearsed situations, during circle time, work time, transition time, and free play. Scenes depict teachers with a variety of teaching styles and skill levels using many different teaching strategies.

Children in the scenes are shown responding in a variety of ways-some are engaged and compliant, some defiant and aggressive. The intent in showing negative as well as positive examples is to demystify the notion of "perfect teaching" and to illustrate how teachers can learn from their mistakes. The video-tapes are used as a catalyst to stimulate group discussion and problem-solving, with the trainer ensuring that the discussion addresses the intended topic and is understood by the teachers. The goal is not only to have teachers grasp the intended concept, but also to have them become actively involved in problemsolving and sharing ideas about the vignette. The trainer can facilitate integration of the concepts by asking how the concepts illustrated in the vignettes apply or don't apply to teachers' own situations.

Using the video-tapes

— Space vignettes throughout the entire day

— Allow for discussion following each vignette. If you are short of time, you may verbally highlight key points in the vignettes. Do not run vignettes together without dialogue.

— Allow teachers' first impressions (insights) to be expressed before you offer analysis and interpretation

— If teachers' reactions are critical of behaviour in the vignette, balance their perspective by noting some positive features of the teachers' behaviours. If you allow a group to be too negative, teachers may feel you could be just as critical of their mistakes.)

— Remember to model a realistic perspective of teaching

— Follow vignette discussions with role-plays to reinforce the key points.

Practice and rehearsal

Practice or rehearsal of unfamiliar or newly-acquired behaviours has been shown to be quite effective in producing behavioural changes. Role-plays help teachers integrate new skills into their repertoires and provide a way for teachers to illustrate particular situations or problems in their classrooms. Teachers doing 10-12 brief role-plays each day of training. It is often best for the trainer to do the first role-play in order to reduce self-consciousness and anxiety. After the trainer has done the first role-plays, we then break the teachers into groups of 2-3 to practice particular skills such as peer-coaching, descriptive commenting, or implementing Time Out in the classroom.

It is a good idea to first instruct teachers to "do it the worst way possible," and then follow this with, "Now use as many of the positive strategies we talked about as possible." The contrast helps reduce performance anxiety over projected demands for perfection and adds humour to the process. Later on, as teachers become more comfortable, they can role-play a situation in front of the whole group-for example, role playing the use of Time-Out with a "difficult child." In this case, one teacher takes the role of the classroom teacher and the rest of the teachers can pretend to be her students. The trainer can help to "freeze frame" the role play and ask the group questions such as, "Now what should she do?" or "What is the child trying to say by behaving like that?"

Homework Assignments

Between training sessions, teachers are given reading and "hands-on" assignments to try the new strategies in their classrooms. The assignments help transfer the training material to the classrooms. They also serve as a stimulus for discussion at the subsequent session. Moreover, assignments convey the critical message that sitting passively in the group is not "magic moondust"; teachers must collaborate with the trainer by trying strategies in their classrooms.

Individual Planning Meetings

It is beneficial for the trainer to schedule an individual planning meeting with each teacher involved in the training. The trainer should meet with the teacher to check in about the teachers' classroom concerns and to help set up individual behaviour plans for more difficult children. If these meetings are scheduled in the teacher's classroom, it also provides the trainer with an opportunity to view the teacher's classroom and teaching environment. These meetings also allow trainers and teachers to get to know one another outside the group and promote engagement with the programme, as well as revealing how well teachers are assimilating the material presented in the group.

While these meetings are recommended when the programme is used as prevention, they are essential when the programme is being used as part of a comprehensive treatment programme for a child with conduct problems. Teachers and trainers collaborate to complete a functional analyses of the target child and to set up an individual behaviour plan. Ideally, the trainer should observe the child in the classroom to obtain a full picture of the challenges that the teacher is facing. The trainer should also facilitate a meeting between the teacher and parents to foster home-school collaboration on the behavioural goals for the child.

Teacher Training Process

Collaborative Training

The training model for working with teachers is active and

collaborative. In a collaborative relationship, the trainer does not set him/herself up as an "expert" dispensing advice about how teachers should teach more effectively. Collaboration implies a reciprocal relationship based on utilising equally the trainer's and the teachers' knowledge, strengths and perspectives. As professionals, both trainers and teachers bring considerable expertise to the training.

Teachers involved in the training have ranged from student teachers who have been in the classroom for only a few months to seasoned teachers with 20 years of classroom experience. They also have varied in their education experience from para-professionals with little formal training to teachers with advanced degrees in education. Together the trainer and teachers form a group of experts with a rich variety of general experience concerning child development, management strategies, and effective teaching methods as well as a wealth of specific experiences from the children in the teachers' current classrooms.

The collaborative trainer actively solicits the teachers' ideas and feelings, learns about their classroom context, and involves them in the learning process by inviting them to share their experiences, discuss their ideas, and engage in problem-solving. Collaboration implies that teachers actively participate in setting goals and the training agenda. Collaboration implies that teachers evaluate each session and the therapist is responsible for incorporating their feedback into subsequent sessions.

Another aspect of the collaborative trainer's job is working with teachers to adapt concepts and skills to the particular circumstances of their classroom and students. For example, a kindergarten teacher with a class of 30 children may need to rely primarily on group incentives whereas a special education teacher with 8 students might use an individual incentive programme tailored to each student's needs. A collaborative trainer also works carefully to process teachers' different theoretical frameworks and to help each teacher to use the principles in a way that is consistent with her teaching style and beliefs. For example, some teachers believe that giving children tangible rewards lowers students' intrinsic motivation.

Although tangible reinforcement is an important part of the classroom management curriculum, the collaborative trainer operates from the assumption that teachers have legitimate grounds for resisting this aspect of the training, would explore alternative ways that these teachers provided their students with positive feedback, and involve the teachers in problem-solving to adapt the concepts to their particular philosophy. It may be that a teacher's objection is based on the idea that she does not want to single out one child for a reward but is comfortable delivering group rewards. These alternate viewpoints can be respected while emphasising the importance of providing some kind of tangible reward for those children who really need one.

A collaborative style of training is demonstrated by open communication patterns within the group and the belief that all teachers provide valuable input. By building a relationship based on rapport with the group, the trainer creates a climate of trust, making the group a safe place for teachers to bring their problems and to risk new approaches. The collaborative trainer is a careful listener. S/he uses open-ended questions to generate discussion and collaboration, and s/he encourages debate and alternative viewpoints, treating all viewpoints with respect. The trainer's empathic understanding is conveyed by the extent to which s/he actively reaches out to the teachers, elicits their ideas, and attempts to understand rather than analyse.

Teacher Training Groups

The essential goal of collaborative training is to "empower" teachers so that they feel confident about their teaching skills and their ability to respond to new situations that may arise. It also reminds them that they have powerful supports in the other teachers in the school and encourages them to make continued use of these links between training sessions. Where necessary, the training can help teachers to problem-solve ways to obtain greater administrative support when they are feeling isolated and overwhelmed. Teachers are also encouraged and helped to take advantage of the support that can be provided when they work to increase parent involvement.

In the training, teachers learn to collaborate in problem-solving, to express their appreciation for each other, and cheer each other's successes in tackling difficult problems. They also learned to share their feelings of guilt, anger, and depression, as well as experiences that involve their own mistakes or misbehavior from their students. These discussions serve as a powerful source of support. Through this sharing of feelings and experiences, commonalty is discovered. Feelings of isolation decrease, and teachers are empowered by the knowledge that they are not alone in their struggles.

Strategies of Trainer

Qualifications of a Trainer

Trainers in the programmes have represented a variety of

disciplines including nursing, social work, education, and psychology. These individuals have masters or doctoral degrees in their professions and a strong background in education, child development, social learning theory, group work, counselling, and clinical work with children and families. The trainers' effectiveness is determined not by their educational or professional background but by their degree of comfort with a collaborative process and their ability to promote intimacy and trust with teachers.

The trainer listens, asks for clarification, is reflective and non judgmental, uses humour, tries to understand what the teacher is saying, helps problem-solve, and does not command, instruct or tell the teacher how to teach. At the same time, the trainer must also be knowledgeable to lead and teach; to explain behavioural principles and provide a clear rationale for them, to challenge teachers to see new perspectives, to elicit the strengths of the teachers in the group, and to provide limit setting within the group when necessary.

Safety of Training Sessions

One of the most difficult aspects of the trainer's role is to prevent the group experience from becoming negative. Consequently, rules to help teachers feel safe and respected are posted on the wall to be added to or referred to if necessary during training sessions. Examples include: (a) only one person may talk at a time; (b) everyone's ideas are respected; (c) anyone has a right to pass; (d) no "put downs" are allowed; and (e) confidentiality within the room.

The group process can be disrupted by a participant who challenges the trainer's knowledge or advocates inappropriate management practices. It is important that the trainer not seem critical or frustrated with this person's comments. Instead the therapist looks for the relevant points in what the person has said and reinforces them for the group. By conveying acceptance and warmth, even towards an obviously difficult group member, the trainer models acceptance and helps group members see that the goal is to understand and respect everyone.

Explanation as Persuasion

Therapeutic change depends on persuasion. This implies that teachers must be given the rationale for each component of the programme. It is important for the trainer to voice clear explanations based upon valid information and knowledge of the developmental literature as well as hard-earned practical wisdom and experience. The treatment principles, objectives and methods should not be shrouded in mystery. If teachers do not understand the rationale for a particular strategy, they may not be motivated to use it in their classrooms.

Reframing

Therapeutic change depends on providing explanatory "stories," alternative explanations that help teachers to reshape their perceptions of and their beliefs about the nature of their problems. Reframing by the trainers or cognitive restructuring is a powerful interpretive tool for helping teachers understand their experiences, thereby promoting change in their behaviours. It involves altering the teacher's emotional and/or conceptual viewpoint of an experience by placing the experience in another "frame" which fits the facts of the situation well, thereby altering its meaning.

One type of reframing frequently use is to re-frame difficulties that a teacher is having with a child in terms of child development. Reframing a difficult child's behaviour in terms of a psychological or emotional drive such as testing the security of limits or moving towards independence, reminds teachers that the behaviour as appropriate or normal. Seen in this light, problematic behaviours are the expression of normal emotions and developmental stages. This attitude enhances coping and decreases feelings of anger and helplessness.

6

Training, Qualifications and Quality

Teacher quality encompasses a range of skills, competencies and motivation. As common sense suggests, specific training is required in order to expect quality services from a teacher or any other skilled professional. Data on training levels are one of the few indicators systematically collected about teachers. This highlights the need for better measures of teacher quality that can be used to compare countries.

Minimum Qualification Standards

There are two issues that make the development of cross-nationally comparable indicators of teacher quality difficult: availability of data and uncertainty about the measurable characteristics of effective teachers. The types of data on teachers that are most widely collected by Ministries of Education, including teachers' academic credentials and whether or not they are certified to teach, are only weakly linked to student achievement in countries where this relationship has been studied.

The teacher quality indicator most often collected is the proportion of trained teachers, or those who have received the minimum organised teacher-training (pre-service or in-

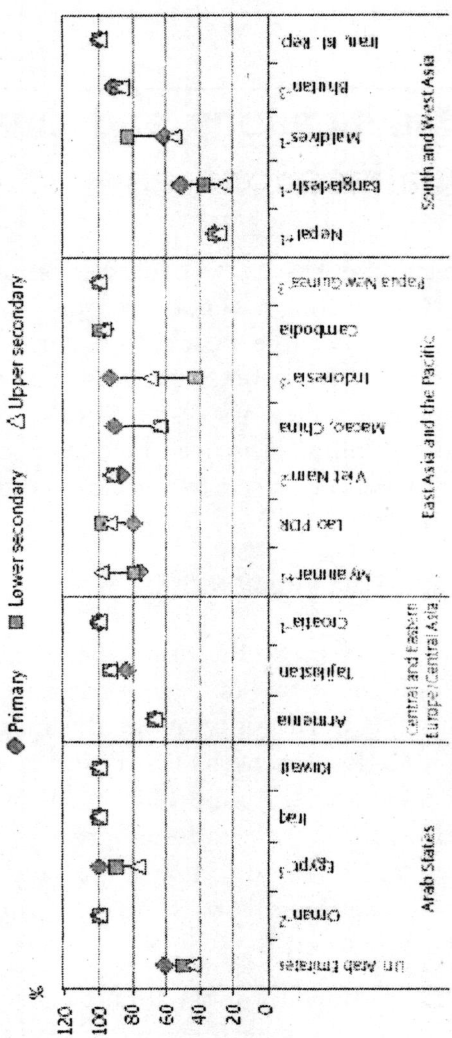

Primary
Lower secondary
Upper secondary
%
120
100
80
60
40
20
0
Un Arab Emirates
Oman[2]
Egypt[1]
Iraq
Kuwait
Armenia
Tajikistan
Croatia[1]
Myanmar[1]
Lao PDR
Viet Nam[2]
Macao, China
Indonesia[2]
Cambodia
Papua New Guinea[2]
Nepal[1]
Bangladesh[1]
Maldives[1]
Bhutan[3]
Iran, Isl. Rep.
Arab States
Central and Eastern Europe/Central Asia
East Asia and the Pacific
South and West Asia

Figure 1

Ctd...

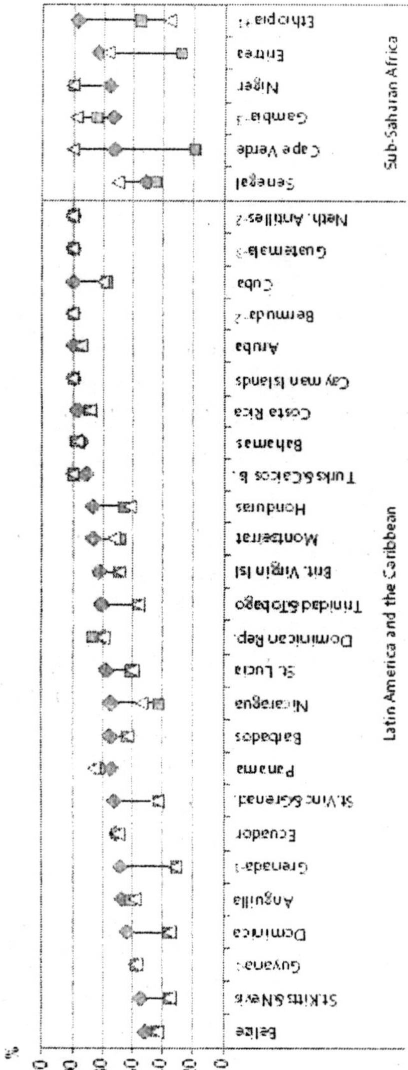

1) Data refer to 2005; 2) Data refer to 2003; 3) Data refer to 2002; 4) Data refer to 2001.

e: UNESCO Institute for Statistics database, 2006.

Figure 1

service) required by a given country figure 1 provides data on the proportion of 'trained' teachers for countries able to provide the measure at primary, lower and upper secondary levels. While useful at the national level, it is limited in terms of cross-national comparisons. The entry standards for teaching vary widely across countries. So this measure points to education systems that fail to meet their own goals or mandates for minimum quality.

There are, in fact, a few countries where less than one-half of teachers reach the standard. It is difficult to use this indicator to measure change over time because countries appearing to have increased their proportion of trained teachers may have simply lowered their standard. Conversely, countries which raise their standard—perhaps to promote the professional profile of teachers—appear as though they have slipped.

Minimum Education for Primary Teacher

Based on data for 106 countries in 2002, the minimum educational level required to teach at the primary level and the proportion of teachers who meet or exceed the standard. In a number of countries, the minimum standard for primary teaching is an upper secondary qualification, typically a specialised programme for training teachers (i.e. ISCED 3C) which is not designed to lead to university studies. For a minority of countries, the standard qualification is equivalent to a lower secondary education (i.e. ISCED 2), which is approximately nine years of basic education. These include Lao PDR in East Asia and the Pacific, the Maldives in South and West Asia and a number of countries in sub-Saharan Africa. Teacher qualification standards at the primary level are generally lower in sub-Saharan Africa than in other regions. Few countries require that teachers earn tertiary-level degrees/diplomas, except in Namibia, South Africa and Zimbabwe. In fact, most countries set a minimum requirement of a post-secondary nontertiary diploma/certificate (ISCED 4) or at least an upper secondary level programme.

Among the sub-Saharan African countries that require an ISCED 4 qualification, Côte d'Ivoire, Gabon, Mauritius and Zambia report that all of their primary teachers meet this standard; only one-quarter of teachers in Guinea have done so. Upper secondary-level qualifications are also very common, especially in Central and Western Africa. To enter into these programmes, trainees must usually have a lower secondary education. But the actual proportion of qualified teachers varies considerably, from 40% in Chad and Guinea-Bissau to 85% in Rwanda.

Finally, minimum standards for primary teachers in Burkina Faso, Congo, Mozambique, Senegal and Tanzania are equivalent to lower secondary education (ISECD 2). A relatively high proportion of teachers meet this low qualification, such as the case of Burkina Faso (87%) and Tanzania (100%) in 2004. In contrast, only about 57% and 60% of primary teachers in Congo and Mozambique completed the minimum training.

However, in many countries female teachers tend to have lower or insufficient qualifications. This can lead to lower earnings according to statutory salary scales and fewer opportunities for promotions to positions of authority and decision-making in the school system. Gender disparities in terms of access to primary teacher training are found in a number of sub-Saharan African countries providing data. In the Congo, 71% of female teachers meet minimum training standards to be a teacher versus 46% of male teachers; similarly 83% of female teachers in Ghana are fully qualified versus 53% of males.

However in Eritrea and Equatorial Guinea, 87% and 89% of male primary teachers have been fully trained versus 68% and 62% of female primary teachers respectively. Access to training is not differentiated by gender in Côte d'Ivoire, Gabon, Mauritius, Tanzania and Zambia. In Namibia, just 38% of primary teachers have been trained but in equal proportions in terms of gender.

Minimum Education for Lower Secondary Teacher

The vast majority of teacher training programmes are either post secondary non-tertiary diplomas/certificates (i.e. ISCED 4) or tertiary level degrees and diplomas (i.e. ISCED 5A and 5B). However, some countries only require upper secondary level teacher training, such as Djibouti in the Arab States; Guinea-Bissau, Mali, Rwanda and Uganda in sub-Saharan Africa; and Vanuatu in the Pacific region. Most countries reporting data had more than one-half of their teachers meeting the respective minimum standard for teaching, but there were exceptions. In Cape Verde just 23% of lower secondary teachers met the required ISCED 5 qualification, followed by Eritrea (31%) and Bangladesh (37%). Meanwhile, among countries with a minimum standard of ISCED 4, only 39% of lower secondary teachers in Saint Kitts and Nevis met the requirement and 26% in Nepal. Finally, for those countries requiring an upper secondary level qualification (ISCED 3), 44% and 9% of teachers have met this minimum standard in Uganda and Mali.

Upper secondary education Most of the 54 countries providing data require a tertiary level qualification to teach at the upper secondary level (Figure 2). In Latin America and the Caribbean, a postsecondary non-tertiary qualification is also required in Antigua and Barbuda,

Belize, Dominica, Guyana and Saint Kitts and Nevis. Most of the countries providing data had more than one-half of all upper secondary teachers meeting the minimum qualifications. However, there are exceptions, including Comoros (45%), Ghana (42%), Belize (41%), Benin (33%), Lebanon (33%), Uganda (32%) and Bangladesh (21%). In some sub-Saharan countries, all upper secondary teachers have reportedly met the minimum qualification standard. However, it is important to note that these countries also demonstrate very low enrolment rates at this level, e.g. only 9% in 2002 in Burkina Faso, where 100% of teachers meet the standard.

While the proportion of teachers who meet the minimum qualification standards highlight gaps in teaching quality between countries, they do not necessarily reflect the education levels held by teachers. This section draws a link through two different sources. One set of comparisons is based on a sample survey of the reading and mathematics teachers of 6th grade students who participated in the 2000-2002 assessment of the Southern and Eastern Africa Consortium for Monitoring Educational Quality (SACMEQ). Data for the second set of comparisons were collected from middle income countries participating in the World Education Indicators (WEI) Programme, coordinated by the UIS and OECD.

The education and training levels of 6thgrade teachers vary considerably across the 13 countries that participated in the SACMEQ study between 2000 and 2002 (Figure 3). From 40% to 97% of 6th grade students in Botswana, Malawi and Tanzaniaare taught reading by teachers holding alower secondary (ISCED 2) qualification or less.

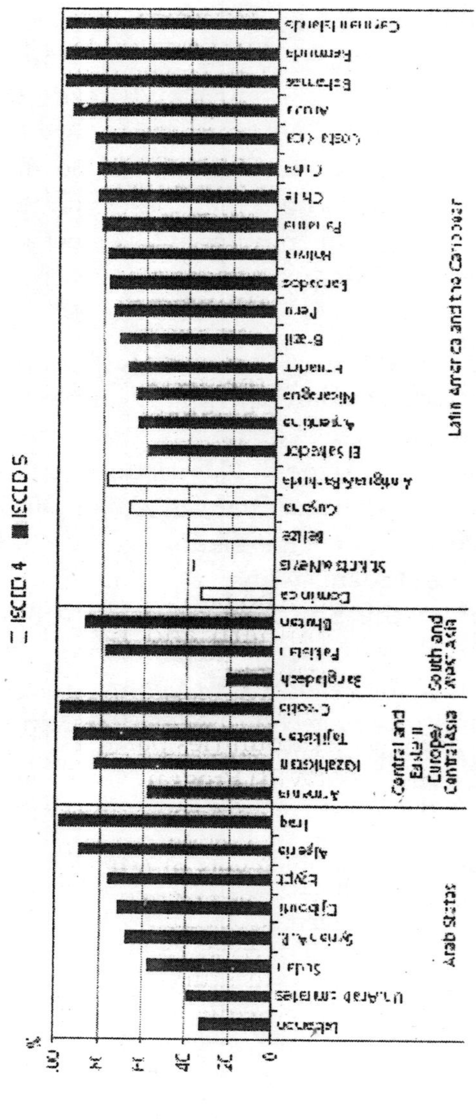

Figure 2

Ctd . . .

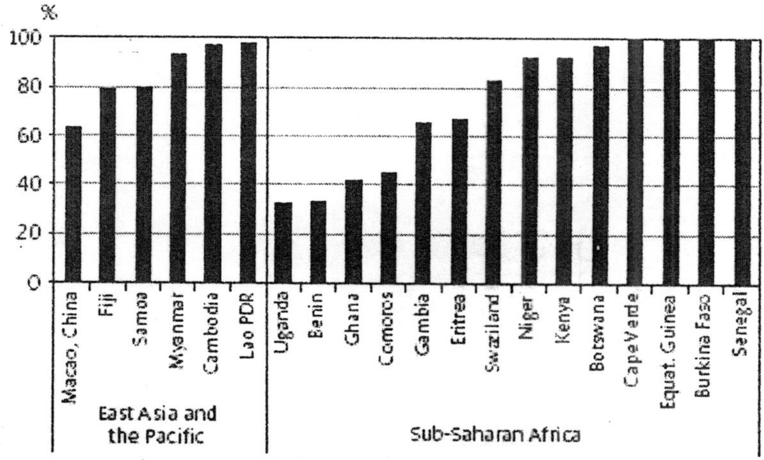

Figure 2

Teacher qualifications are low in Lesotho, where more than one-half of 6th grade students are taught reading by teachers with only a primary level education not much more than the students they teach. At the other end of the spectrum, Mauritius, Seychelles, South Africa and Swaziland have at least 45% of their teachers with A-level (ISCED 3A) or tertiary level qualifications.

While relatively few of the 6th grade pupils have reading teachers with only a lower secondary qualification or less in Mauritius, Seychelles and Swaziland (1.6%, 8.3% and 12.8% respectively), over 30% of teachers in South Africa have only this level of education. In order to increase substantially the number of teachers with at least a lower secondary qualification in Lesotho and Tanzania, for example, more students need to complete that level of education. In 2003, less than 20% of children in Tanzania even began lower secondary education. This was the case

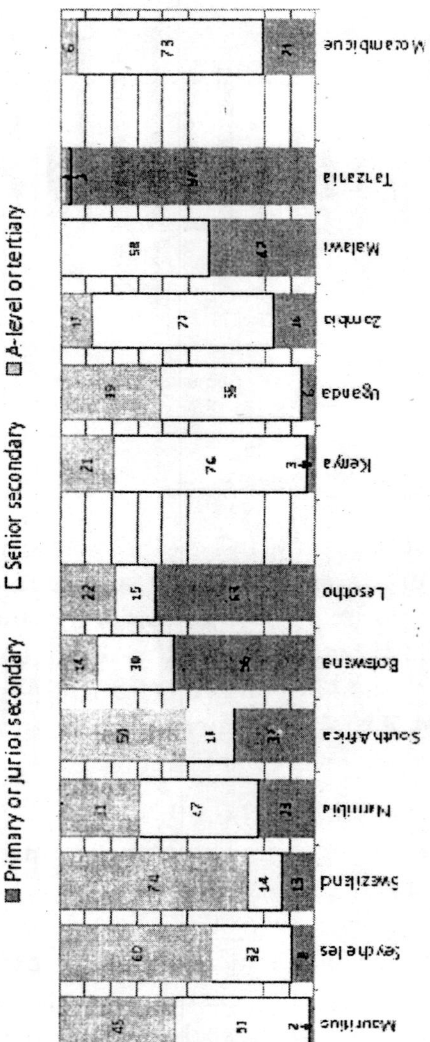
Primary or junior secondary
Senior secondary
A-level or tertiary
Mauritius
Seychelles
Swaziland
Namibia
South Africa
Botswana
Lesotho
Kenya
Uganda
Zambia
Malawi
Tanzania
Mozambique

Figure 3

for less than 50% of secondary school-age children in Lesotho.

In Malawi, less than one-third of all students who start primary school complete it. These factors limit the pool of potential primary teachers with higher level qualifications. Lesotho faces relatively little pressure to expand teaching forces to meet UPE by 2015 and, therefore, could try to raise qualification levels. But it will be far more difficult to balance these two goals in Tanzania, where educational demand will increase.

Figure 3 shows a wide distribution among 6th grade students in terms of their teachers' educational qualifications in Southern and Eastern Africa. Figure 4 shows this distribution by type of location (rural, small town or large city). According to the data, 6th grade students appear to be just as likely to have a teacher with at least a junior secondary qualification (lower secondary) if they live in a rural community or a large city in nearly all of the countries participating in SACMEQ. However, the opposite is true in some cases.

In South Africa, 37% of 6th grade students in rural communities and small towns are likely to be taught reading by teachers with at leasta lower secondary qualification compared to 17% in large cities. Access to more highly trained teachers—in this case reading teachers with at least an A-level qualification was also equitably distributed among schools in urban and rural locations, with the exceptions of Botswana, Namibia and South Africa. Moreover, the data suggest that 6th graders outside of large cities are more likely to have a teacher with high qualifications in Mauritius, Swaziland and Uganda, which may reflect policies to post newly-qualified teachers to rural areas. It is important to note that there may be very uneven

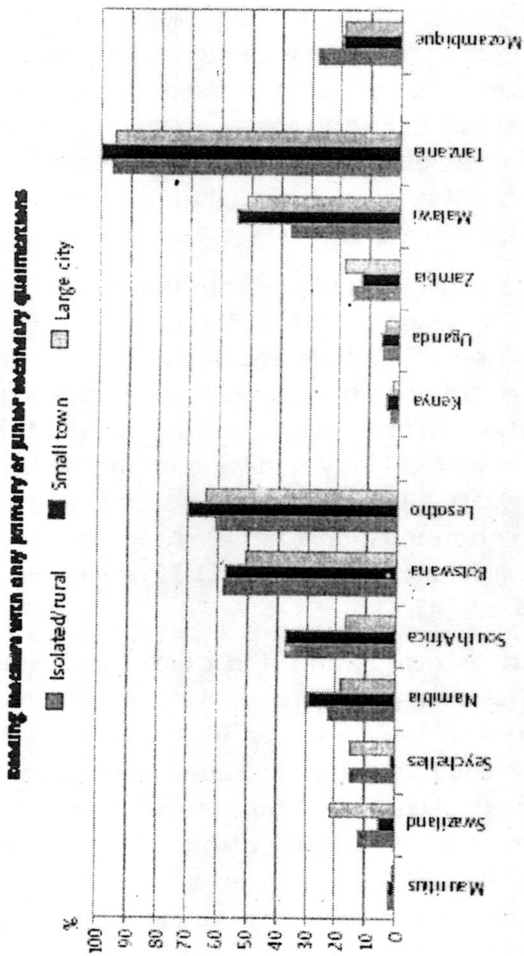
Isolated/rural
Small town
Large city
%
100
90
80
70
60
50
40
30
20
10
0
Mauritius
Swaziland
Seychelles
Namibia
SouthAfrica
Botswana
Lesotho
Kenya
Uganda
Zambia
Malawi
Tanzania
Mozambique

Figure 4

Ctd . . .

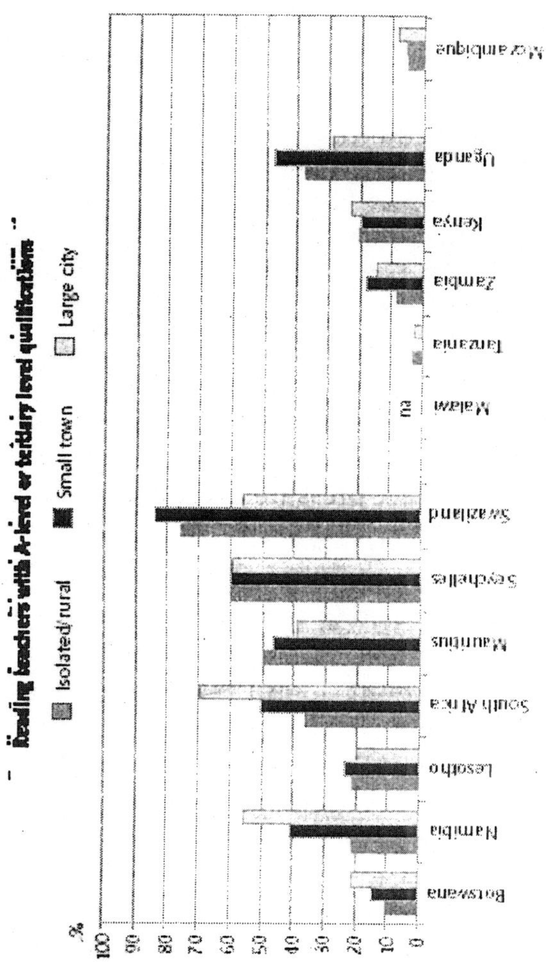
Reading teachers with A-level or tertiary level qualifications
Isolated/rural
Small town
Large city
%
100
90
80
70
60
50
40
30
20
10
0
Botswana
Namibia
Lesotho
South Africa
Mauritius
Seychelles
Swaziland
Malawi
na
Tanzania
Zambia
Kenya
Uganda
Mozambique

Figure 4

distributions of qualified teachers within the districts of either a rural or urban zone. For example, in Lesotho two-thirds or more of 6th grade students were taught by teachers with only a primary education in the Mafeteng, Qacha's Nek and Maseru districts. This was the case for less than one-quarter of students in the districts of Quthing and Butha-Buthe.

Teacher experience also varies considerably by school location in SACMEQ countries. Research suggests that students learn more from experienced teachers than they do from those less experienced. But the benefits of experience appear to level off after five years. Studies in the United States suggest that there are no noticeable differences, for example, in the effectiveness of teachers with five versus ten years of experience. The percentage of 6th grade students whose reading teacher has less than three years of experience, by the location of the school. The gap between rural and urban areas was highest in Malawi, Mozambique and Uganda, which all face pressure to expand the number of primary teachers to reach UPE.

Individual studies conducted in sub-regions or other parts of sub-Saharan Africa, however, suggest larger problems attracting qualified teachers to work in rural areas. For example, Morgan et al. found critical shortages in science and mathematics teachers in the South African province of KwaZulu-Natal, where more than 300 secondary schools were not even offering these subjects. A recent study in Mali found that 58% of urban teachers have completed the required four-year programme of upper secondary education, but only 31% of rural teachers had done the same. A different pattern emerges in Burkina Faso, where 58% of primary teachers in urban areas hold a primary teacher's college certificate. Yet, as many as four out of ten in this group have also completed a university-level credential. In contrast, 89% of primary teachers in rural regions hold teaching certificates but almost none of them have university credentials (ibid). Some countries have implemented policies aimed at reducing regional imbalances in teacher quality.

For example, Ghana has attempted to attract qualified teachers and head teachers to rural regions using incentive packages, which provided free bicycles to facilitate travel, for example, and free or low-cost housing. At the same time, the government also instituted additional redeployment policies, such as the transfer of excess office staff to rural classrooms and more use of double-shifting. The government also implemented the National Service Scheme programme, whereby university graduates had to complete a year of teaching in classrooms before they could be offered employment. This programme was later expanded to new graduates from Polytechnics and other institutions of post-secondary education, and the length of required service was extended to two years. While this innovative programme brought more teachers to classrooms, it did not ensure a minimum level of professional training.

Such teacher allocation policies have proven to minimise variation by socioeconomic status (SES) of pupils. Even though teacher qualifications varied among countries participating in SACMEQ, high and low SES students were equally likely to be assigned to teachers with relatively high or low educational qualifications in most participating countries. For example, students with high and low SES were equally likely to be taught reading by teachers with a lower secondary qualification or less in most countries. Access to more highly trained teachers was inequitably distributed between high and low SES students in only three countries—Mauritius, Namibia and South Africa—although these gaps were wide.

In Mauritius and Namibia, high SES 6th grade students were more than twice as likely to be taught reading by a teacher holding at least an A-level qualification than were low SES students. This was also the case in South Africa but to a lesser extent. WEI programme highlight differences in teacher qualifications among middle income countries throughout the world. One pattern emerges across the countries: teacher qualifications continue to rise over time. All countries increased the number of teachers with tertiary qualifications between 1995 and 2003, although Brazil, Egypt and Indonesia must make considerable progress before all teachers hold this degree.

In Indonesia, for instance, more than 90% of preprimary teachers hold an upper secondary qualification, while at the primary level approximately 50% of teachers have completed tertiary level training. The majority of pre-primary teachers in Brazil and Malaysia also have either a 'standard' upper secondary education or have completed a pre-university preparation programme. While the former type of programme offers certain educational benefits to future teachers (such as access to university-level programmes), the latter tends to focus more on pedagogical skills and includes a 'practice teaching' component.

The majority of pre-primary and primary teachers in Chile, Jamaica and Thailand held tertiary level qualifications in 2002. In contrast, the majority of teachers at these levels held upper secondary qualifications in Brazil, China and Malaysia. While almost all primary teachers in Thailand have at least a tertiary qualification (i.e. 5A or 5B), only 27% in Brazil and China have earned similar levels of education. In Malaysia only 4% of primary teachers have achieved tertiary level education, but most of them have completed a vocational programme at the secondary level. In Tunisia, 77% of primary teachers have completed a post-secondary non-tertiary programme (ISCED 4), but none have a tertiary level education.

In contrast, the vast majority of primary teachers (92%) in Zimbabwe held tertiary level qualifications. Lower and upper secondary levels of education are characterised by rising educational qualifications among teachers. For instance, all lower and upper secondary teachers in Indonesia and Thailand have completed a tertiary level diploma or degree, while three-quarters of secondary teachers in Malaysia have achieved the same. Tunisia, on the other hand, recruits many upper secondary and post-secondary (non-tertiary) teachers with qualifications similar to those of their students. This situation raises questions about whether teachers can meet their students' learning needs.

Research studies have shown positive associations between student achievement and teachers' academic skills, level of content knowledge, years of experience and participation in content-related professional development opportunities. Yet, unfortunately, the administrative data bases of education ministries generally do not include or maintain these kinds of measures. A number of these measures have been administered, to differing degrees, as part of international assessments of students. For example, data on whether students are taught mathematics by teachers who have an academic qualification in the subject were collected as part of the TIMSS and SACMEQ data collections, while data on teachers' participation levels in professional development activities were collected in TIMSS, PIRLS and SACMEQ. SACMEQ is unique by allowing a direct comparison of students' background characteristics and their teachers' academic skills in mathematics and reading.

Research shows that students tend to learn more from teachers with strong rather than weak academic skills. However, some researchers argue that the quality of instruction has more to do with teachers' performance in the classroom than on standardised tests. Yet, it is very difficult to measure many of the traits associated with effective teaching, such as interpersonal and public speaking skills, in addition to enthusiasm for working with children. Most studies examining the link between student learning and teacher skills tend to focus exclusively on academic skills. As part of the SACMEQ study, 6th grade reading and mathematics teachers were tested in their respective fields of instruction. Their average scores were then compared to those of their students (by mapping both sets of scores at the same scale, with the student mean equal to 500 and a standard deviation equal to 100).

The reading scores of teachers ranged from an average of 695 in Uganda to about 800 or above in Kenya and Seychelles (teachers in South Africa and Mauritius did not take the assessments). Variation within countries were of similar magnitude, with the scores ranging from 120 to 150 points in most countries. Tanzania had the least variation among teachers' scores, with 95% of teachers scoring within a range of 87 points; in Uganda there was a gap of 220 points. Moreover, a number of countries had a sizeable overlap between the reading scores of 6th grade students and their reading teachers.

For example, the highest performing students in Seychelles, Tanzania and Uganda scored similar levels to that of the average teacher in their country. The range in the mathematics scores of teachers was even wider, both within and between countries. Mathematics teachers in Kenya and Seychelles had the highest average scores (as they did in reading) and teachers in Namibia had the lowest. Teachers performed, on average, better in mathematics than in reading.

Reading and math achievement scores of 6th grade teachers were not strongly associated with school location (isolated/rural, small town or large city) in most countries (Figure 5). For example, only in Namibia, Tanzania and Uganda did teachers in large cities score significantly higher in mathematics than those in isolated or rural areas. In most other SACMEQ countries, urban and rural teachers had similar mathematics results. But there were two interesting exceptions: in Malawi and the Seychelles, students in isolated/rural areas had teachers with higher math scores than those in large cities.Using the SACMEQ data, it is possible to explore the relationship between teachers' education levels and their academic skills.

In most SACMEQ countries, there was a positive relationship between 6th grade teachers' education allevels and their academic skills in reading and math (Figure 6). On average, reading teachers with an A-level or tertiary qualification scored about 40 points higher than those with a lower secondary or primary degree. Differences were statistically significant in all countries except Malawi, Tanzania and Uganda. However, test scores among 6thgrade math teachers did not vary significantly by education level in Kenya, Mozambique, and Uganda.While an improvement over administrative data, these measures are inadequate to monitor cross-national trends in teacher quality. The different regional and international studies cover different grades, across different countries, using different measures and sampling frames. They are useful for obtaining a snapshot of teacher quality. However, measures derived from these sources have not been collected in a sufficiently comparable way over a sufficiently long period of time to clearly identify trends in teacher quality.

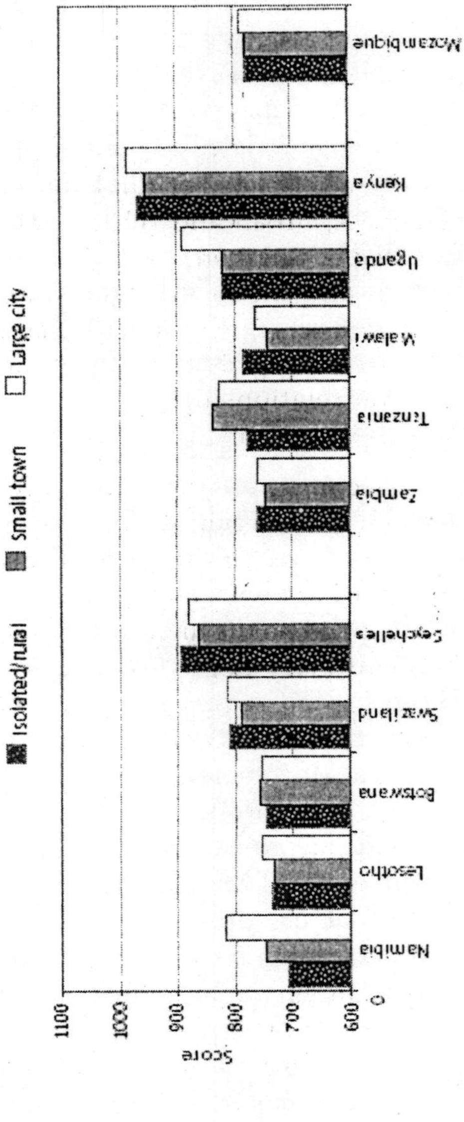
Isolated/rural
Small town
Large city
Score
1100
1000
900
800
700
600
0
Namibia
Lesotho
Botswana
Swaziland
Seychelles
Zambia
Tanzania
Malawi
Uganda
Kenya
Mozambique

Figure 5

Ctd . . .

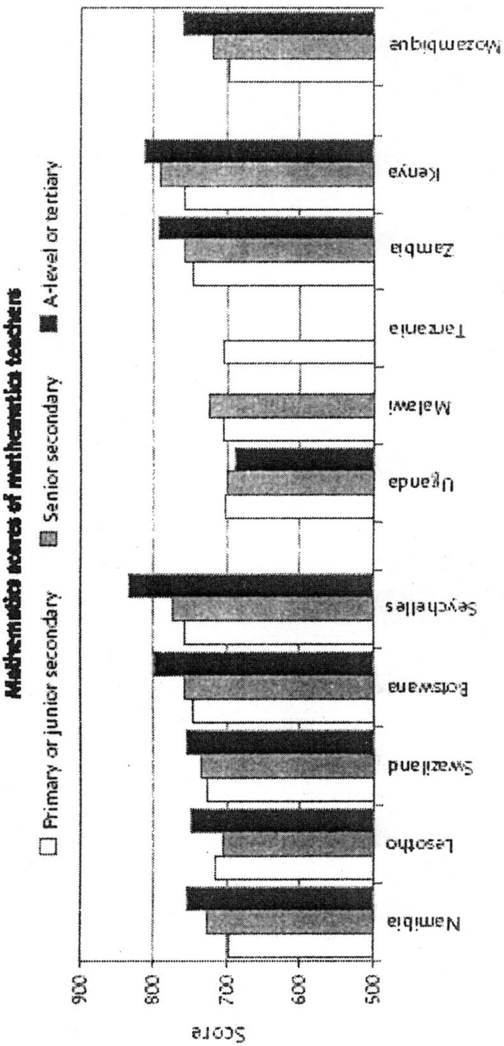
Mathematics scores of mathematics teachers
Primary or junior secondary
Senior secondary
A-level or tertiary
Score
900
800
700
600
500
Namibia
Lesotho
Swaziland
Botswana
Seychelles
Uganda
Malawi
Tanzania
Zambia
Kenya
Mozambique

Figure 6

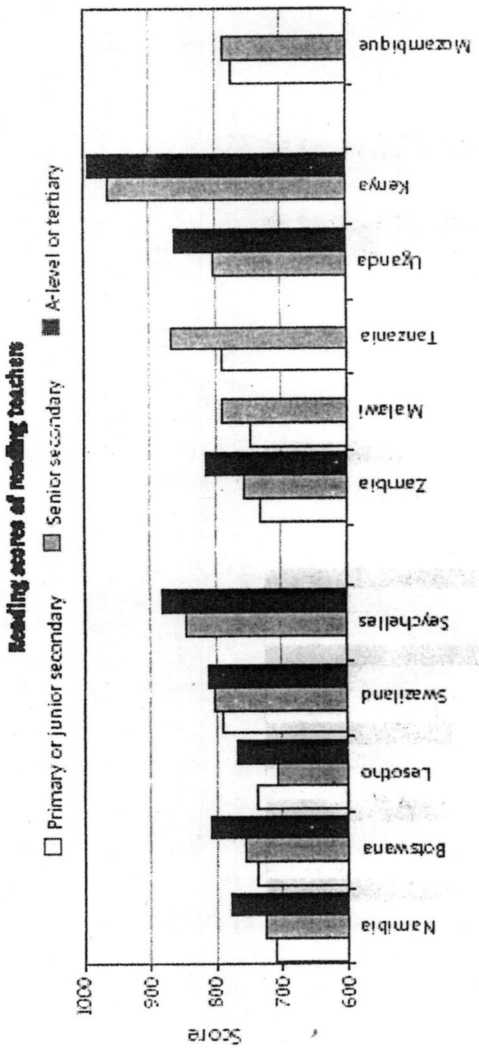
Reading scores of reading teachers
Primary or junior secondary
Senior secondary
A-level or tertiary
Score
1000
900
800
700
600
Namibia
Botswana
Lesotho
Swaziland
Seychelles
Zambia
Malawi
Tanzania
Uganda
Kenya
Mozambique

Figure 6

Even with stable longitudinal measures of teachers' academic skills, content knowledge and experience, current research suggests that these measures explain a relatively small proportion of the variation in achievement that is associated with the assignment of a student to a particular teacher. For equity reasons, it is important to monitor whether poor and wealthy students, taught in urban and rural schools, living in high-income and low-income countries have equal access to teachers. But even policies to balance these measures will not fully close the gaps in achievement between advantaged and disadvantaged students.

IMPROVING EDUCATIONAL BACKGROUND OF TEACHERS

Teachers, like other skilled workers, benefit from on-the-job training, which is commonly referred to as continuing professional development (CPD). Relevant activities can include: improving teachers' general education background, as well as their knowledge and understanding of the subjects they teach; instruction on how children learn different subjects; developing practical skills and competencies; learning new teaching strategies and how to use new technologies; improved professionalism and ethics; in addition to providing knowledge and skills linked to the ever-changing needs of a dynamic society.

Participation in professional development activities has been shown to have a significant positive impact on teachers' beliefs and practices, students' learning and on the implementation of educational reforms. Unfortunately, there are very little cross-nationally comparable data on teachers' participation in CPD. However, data from sample surveys of teachers, including SACMEQ and IEA's

(International Association for the Evaluation of Educational Achievement) Progress in International Reading Literacy Study (PIRLS), can indicate the degree to which different countries use CPD to maintain and improve the quality of their teaching forces.

Professional development activities are not systematically more common in high-income than middle- or lower-income countries; teacher participation varies within each. Among the lower middle- and lower-income countries that participated in PIRLS, only the Former Yugoslav Republic of Macedonia, Romania and the Russian Federation each had more than 60% of 4th graders whose teachers had less than six hours of CPD during the previous two years, while Iran had only 27%. In contrast, over 35% of teachers in Iran, Morocco and Turkey participated in 16 hours or more of workshops or seminars over this period. Among upper middle- and high-income countries, France had the largest proportion of 4th graders (86%) whose teachers had virtually no CPD over the previous two years, while Israel, Italy, Latvia, Hungary, Singapore, Slovenia and the United States each had 34% or more of their students at this level taught by teachers with over 16 hours of CPD in the previous two years.

While relatively few lower middle- andlow-income countries participated in thePIRLS study, data from the SACMEQ studycan help fill this gap. Participation rates in CPD varied widely within and between the SACMEQ countries. Forexample, two-thirds or more of 6th grade reading teachers in Malawi, Mozambique and Tanzania reported no CPD participation in the previous three years. But nearly two thirds or more of these teachers had done so in Botswana, Namibia, South Africa and Uganda. Low participation rates may reflect a lack of CPD offerings or that uncertified teachers are not eligible, as in the case of Zambia.

There was also variation among countries with higher rates of participation. While all 13 SACMEQ countries had at least 10% of their students taught by reading teachers with 16 hours or more of in-service training, the figure was over 25% in Botswana, Lesotho, Namibia, South Africa, Uganda and Zambia. Patterns of participation were similar for mathematics teachers. Teachers in rural regions may find it more difficult to participate in CPD, given the expense and time required to travel.

Yet, this does not appear to be a statistically significant factor, according to SACMEQ data. Figure 1 shows the percentage of 6th grade students whose reading teachers reported participating in CPD activities in the previous three years. For example, Kenya had a greater proportion of urban students (45%) taught by teachers with in service training compared to 20% of rural students. In Tanzania, 6th grade students were considerably more likely to be taught by a reading teacher with recent in-service training if they lived in a rural area or small town than in a large city.

This does not mean that distance from major population centres is not important. An earlier wave of SACMEQ data demonstrate how regional disparities in training opportunities may exist within countries, particularly between urban and rural regions.

Teachers' participation in CPD does not necessarily translate into improvements in students' learning. Critics contend that if professional development focuses too much on process (e.g. how to teach) and not enough on content (e.g. how children learn), student learning will not necessarily improve. Individual country studies suggest that in most parts of the world the majority of CPD activities are "too short, too unrelated to the needs of teachers and too ineffective to upgrade teaching knowledge". Little data are available, however, to compare the content of professional development activities.

Of the 44% of teachers participating in CPD, just one in four rated the activities as effective or very effective in Seychelles; in South Africa and Uruguay, only one in two. Yet, over 80% of teachers did so in Malawi and Tanzania. These data suggest the need to improve both access to and quality of professional development activities in Southern and Eastern Africa—and may be broadly suggestive of the same issue in other less-developed regions.

7

Teacher Quality in Teaching

Many of the new ideas and new funds are directed at the issue of improving teacher quality. For many years, research has found teacher quality to be a key determinant of student success. Large-scale studies suggest that teacher quality is more closely related to student achievement than other factors, such as class size, spending and instructional materials. As part of his landmark 1966 study, *Equality of Educational Opportunity*, sociologist James Coleman noted that among African American students, there was a correlation between student achievement and teachers scores on vocabulary tests. Among students generally, however, Coleman found no discernable pattern.

But Coleman's evaluation was aggregated at the school level, meaning important variations among individual teachers and classrooms within the same school were not measured. In recent years, a new approach to measuring teacher quality has been developed, focusing on the value that teachers provide to individual students in their classrooms. By testing students annually and comparing the growth of individual students and individual classrooms, researchers can pinpoint the effect teachers are having on their students. Because the analysis is focused on learning gains, and not absolute test scores, the influence of background characteristics like socioeconomic status can be parsed out. Not surprisingly, researchers have found that some teachers are much more effective than others.

Value-added measures also permit researchers to examine the cumulative effects a string of high-quality versus low-quality teachers can have on student performance over several years. Some of the best research on this subject has been done by statistician William Sanders in Tennessee. The state of Tennessee evaluates all of its teachers based on the learning gains individual students make while in their respective classrooms. Using this information, Sanders categorised the state's teachers into quintiles based on the performance of their students. As part of his research, he tracked two comparable sets of third-graders: one group which had three successive teachers from the top quintile, and the other that had three successive teachers from the bottom quintile.

Importance of Verbal Ability and Content Knowledge

Teachers verbal ability appears to be especially important at the elementary level, perhaps because this is when children typically learn to read. Stanford University economist Eric Hanushek, who has conducted extensive academic literature reviews on teacher quality, said, "[P]erhaps the closest thing to a consistent conclusion across studies is the finding that teachers who perform well on verbal ability tests do better in the class-room [in boosting student achievement]".

More recent studies suggest that subject-matter background can also have a positive effect on student performance. Research has generally shown that high school math and science teachers who have a major in the subjects they teach elicit greater gains from their students than out-of-field teachers, controlling for student's prior academic achievement and socioeconomic status. These same studies also suggest that possessing an undergraduate major in math and science has a greater positive effect on student performance than certification in those subjects. Research has not always produced consistent results on the effects of teachers having a master's degree, but in the better designed studies the effects are weak, at best.

In US, yet even as research demonstrates the importance of content knowledge, new data from the National Center for Education Statistics (NCES) suggests that too many students, especially in the middle-school grades, have teachers who are not fully qualified in their subject areas. For example, in 1999-2000, 15 to 22 percent of middle-grade students in English, math and science had teachers who lacked a post-secondary major, minor or certification in the subject taught. In biology and life science, physical science and English as a Second Language (ESL) or bilingual education classes, the data are even more troubling. Between 30 and 40 percent of middle-grade students had teachers who lacked a major, minor or certification in these subjects.

Knowledge of Pedagogy and Education Degrees

The verbal ability and content knowledge of teachers have been linked to higher student achievement, but what about other attributes, like knowledge of pedagogy, degrees in education or amount of time spent practice teaching? After all, these are the requirements that make up the bulk of current teacher certification regimes. There is a great deal of contention surrounding the evidence on these components, with some studies linking these requirements to improved student achievement. However, the quality of many of these studies has been called into question. A report by the Abell Foundation evaluated approximately 175 studies spanning the past 50 years, all of which purported to demonstrate a connection between certification and improved student out-comes. The analysis found that virtually all of these evaluations were not scientifically rigorous, did not use generally accepted statistical techniques to gather data and relied too much on anecdotal evidence.

Scientific evidence also raises questions about the value of attendance in schools of education. In a recent study, economists Dan Goldhaber and Dominic Brewer found that while certified math and science teachers outperformed those who lack certification, there was no statistical difference in performance between teachers who attended conventional training programs and received traditional teaching licenses versus those who did not complete such programs and were teaching on emergency or temporary certificates.

Preparing Qualified Teachers

Briefly charting the history of teacher preparation is instructive in learning how the United States arrived at its current model. While state-approved teacher preparation programmes are the norm throughout the nation today, this has not always been the case. It was only after the Civil War that most states required teachers to pass a locally administered examination to receive a state certificate, typically including a test in basic skills, but also in U.S. history, geography, spelling and grammar. Still, the state role in teacher preparation was kept to a minimum, with no uniform approach to teacher certification applied in the 19th century.

Around the turn of the century, however, relatively small teachers colleges and departments of pedagogy at some of the nation's universities were converted into undergraduate and graduate schools of education. These revamped institutions developed specialisations in fields such as school administration, curriculum development and educational psychology. As historians David Angus and Diane Ravitch have argued, the creation of schools of education marked a turning point in the history of American education. The formal establishment of schools of education had two reverberating effects: the division between classroom teachers and teacher educators, and the formalised split between pedagogy and the traditional disciplines of the liberal arts and sciences.

Whereas history, English and science departments stressed the importance of subject-area knowledge for teachers, the new leaders of the teaching profession in schools of education and teacher colleges stressed the importance of courses in pedagogy and passing related tests. Authority over teacher certification was increasingly focused at the state level, and its substance was increasingly focused on the completion of teacher education programs. This replaced the former system, which had emphasised local certificates and the passing of subject-matter examinations.

Leaders in the teaching profession sought to boost the professional image and prestige of teaching, seeking to elevate it to the status of law or medicine, by controlling entry into the teaching ranks through increasingly prescriptive state laws and regulations. Did the reforms improve the prestige of the profession and the quality of the teaching force? Judging by today's data, it seems they did not.

Researches emphasises the importance of recruiting teachers with solid content knowledge and verbal ability, but today's certification system seems to work against the recruitment of these individuals. Of course, many teachers are smart and know their subjects well, but our system allows too many poorly qualified individuals into the classroom while creating barriers for the most talented candidates. While 99 percent of teachers possess bachelors degrees and 52 percent have graduate degrees, according to recent data from the National Center for Education Statistics (NCES), only 38 percent have an undergraduate or graduate degree in an academic field outside of a school of education (Table 1). Even at the high school level, where most of the curriculum is focused on the academic disciplines, a full third of teachers in the United States lack a degree in an academic field.

Table 1. Recent of full-time public school teachers who majored in various fields of study for a bachelor's or graduate degree, by selected school and teacher characteristics

School characteristic	*Academic field*	*Subject area education*	*General education*	*Other education*
All targeted public school teachers	38	18	37	7
School instructional level				
Elementary school	22	9	58	11
Middle school	44	22	27	7
High school	66	29	5	1
Combined	55	35	8	2
Teaching experience				
3 or fewer years	50	11	37	2

4 to 9 years	41	16	39	5
10 to 19 years	32	20	37	11
20 or more years	36	20	36	8

The same data reveal that the remaining 62 percent of teachers have degrees in education-related subjects, typically obtained through schools of education and teacher-training programmes. Historically, research suggests that students enrolled in schools of education are not as academically accomplished as other university students. One such study, conducted by Education Week, tracked the top quartile of 1992-1993 college graduates, and found that just 14 percent entered some type of teacher-preparation program, only 12 percent actually taught, and a mere 11 percent stayed in the teaching profession through 1997.

Similar data from NCES also suggest that schools of education fail to attract the best students. For example, among college graduates who majored in education, just 14 percent had SAT or ACT scores in the top quartile, compared to 26 percent who majored in the social sciences and 37 percent who majored in mathematics, computer science, or the natural sciences. In contrast, 25 percent of uncertified teachers scored in the top quartile on these tests, as did 33 percent of private-school teachers (Figure 1).

Some of the difficulty with attracting the best students may lie with the rigidity of training programs and at least partial dissatisfaction among teachers with the content of such programs. As University of Virginia assistant professor Frederick Hess observes, other professions that employ highly qualified recent college graduates, such as management consulting or journalism, use a flexible approach to hiring, recruiting students from a variety of fields. However, schools of education firmly control the entry process into teaching, as most states require completion of a number of education school courses in order to qualify for certification.

Also, there are significant opportunity costs associated with teaching that simply do not exist in other professions. Because the typical undergraduate education major requires several semesters of courses, prospective teachers must decide relatively early in their academic careers that teaching is the field they wish to pursue. If they realise during their junior or senior years that they wish to enter teaching, candidates typically have to enrol in one to two years of graduate study and spend thousands more dollars on tuition, books, supplies and other expenses.

As Hess points out, candidates must sacrifice the opportunity to work while attending classes, endure additional certification requirements if they attempt to teach outside of the state in which their training program is located and must practice teach for extended periods of time with little or no pay. This process imposes significant costs on highly qualified candidates with a variety of career options. Other fields that may offer more generous compensation do not erect these added barriers, which only drive up the costs associated with teaching. These barriers to entry are particularly onerous for many highly skilled minority candidates with other career possibilities, who may be discouraged from teaching because of the financial costs of enrolling in a preparation program.

Furthermore, the teacher compensation system discourages interested candidates from entering teaching. Teacher pay scales negotiated at the local level are typically based on seniority and the number of credentials that teachers possess. While beginning employees in every profession typically earn less than their more experienced colleagues, employees in nearly every other field often qualify for bonuses, based in large measure on their job performance. Moreover, employees in these professions often have more opportunities to advance based upon hard work and exceptional performance. Unfortunately, teaching does not reward performance, innovation or creativity; teachers gradually move up the pay ladder year by year, regardless of what takes place in their classrooms.

The most talented prospective teachers might also be discouraged by the lack of rigor of the courses offered in many schools of education. A majority of graduates of schools of education believe that traditional teacher preparation programs left them ill prepared for the challenges and rigours of the classroom. According to NCES data, fewer than 36 percent of new teachers feel "very well prepared" to implement curriculum and performance standards, less than 30 percent feel prepared to integrate technology into instruction and less than 20 percent feel prepared to meet the needs of diverse students or those with limited English proficiency.

Teacher Preparation and Certification

An interesting innovation has developed in recent years that points the way toward a more promising system of teacher preparation and certification. Alternate routes to certification, as opposed to the traditional routes offered by colleges of education, streamline the process of certification to move qualified candidates into the classroom on a fast-track basis. Interested individuals must pass the same certification or licensure exams as their traditionally certified peers, but many of the other requirements—course work in education philosophy or methods, pedagogy, practice teaching, etc.—are often shortened or waived entirely.

Many times, extra support is given to these new teachers once they are in the classroom. By reducing the barriers to entry, these programs enlarge the pool of potential teachers. One argument made against alternate routes is that they attract teachers who do not intend to stay in teaching for the long term. Yet initial evidence suggests that retention rates for teachers certified through alternate routes are higher than for teachers who enter the classroom through traditional routes. Nationwide, about 85 percent of teachers certified through alternate routes remain in the classroom five years later, demonstrating that truncated training programs with highly qualified candidates do not result in those same teachers leaving the profession early in their careers.

In many states, alternate routes are popular career choices among candidates from racial or ethnic minority groups. In Texas for example, while 91 percent of all teachers are white, 41 percent of teachers entering through alternate routes are from minority groups. Moreover, retention rates are higher for African American teachers who entered teaching through an alternate route as compared to their traditionally certified peers. Teachers certified through alternate routes in Texas are also more likely to pass the state's initial certification exam on the first try.

In California, just under a third of the state's new teachers in 2000-2001 were teachers certified through alternate routes. Ethnic minorities compose about 46 percent of this group of teachers, compared to approximately 25 percent of the overall teacher force. In addition, between 25 and 40 percent of graduates from the state's traditional teacher-training programmes do not take teaching jobs in the state's schools, while about 87 percent of teachers who are hired as interns remain in the profession after three years.

There are several well-known programs nationwide that recruit highly qualified candidates using alternate routes, including the Troops to Teachers program. This program provides financial assistance and training to retiring military personnel and helps to place them in local school districts, thus providing a new source of teachers to schools in 20 states. According to the National Center for Education Information, teachers certified through alternate routes bring diversity to the classroom and are more apt to take challenging assignments.

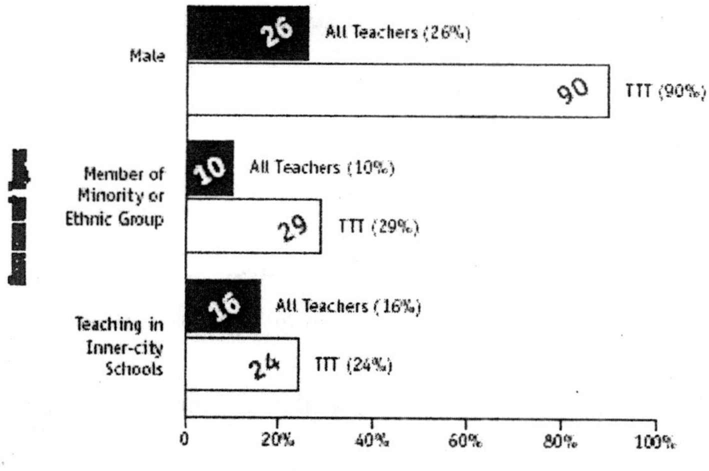

Figure 2. Characteristics of Troops to Teachers (TTT) Compared with the overall teaching force

Ninety percent of teachers in the Troops to Teachers program are male, compared to just 26 percent in the overall teaching force. About 30 percent of teachers in the program are from a minority or ethnic group, compared to just 10 percent overall. These teachers are also placed in high-demand subject areas, with 29 percent teaching math and 24 percent teaching in the sciences, while 11 percent were special education teachers. About 25 percent were teaching in inner-city schools, compared to 16 percent overall nationwide (figure 2 and 3).

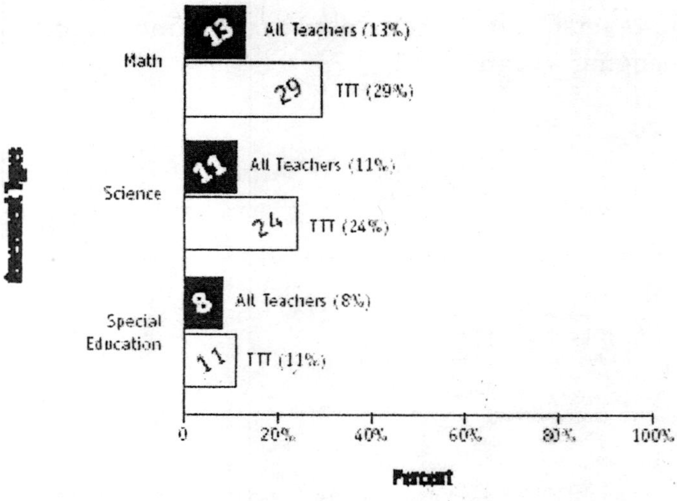

Figure 3. Subjects Taught by Troops to Teachers (TTT) Versus all Teachers

Another popular and successful program associated with alternate routes to teaching is Teach For America (TFA). This nationwide nonprofit organisation recruits accomplished college graduates without formal backgrounds in education to teach in high-need urban and rural schools. Candidates apply to the program and, if selected, attend a summer training course before being placed in school districts across the country. Teach for America and the host school districts provide new teachers with support during the two-year program, after which some teachers return to graduate school, transfer to other professions or continue teaching. Since its inception in 1989, TFA has placed more than 8,000 talented young men and women in our nation's neediest schools.

One of the largest districts using TFA teachers is the Houston Independent School District, which has been involved with the program since 1993. A recent study conducted by the Center for Research on Education Outcomes evaluated the performance of TFA teachers in Houston from 1996 to 2000. The study examined the effect of the average TFA teacher on student test scores compared to the average non-TFA teacher and compared the best and worst TFA teachers to the best and worst non-TFA teachers.

The evaluation found that, on average, across different grades and subjects, the effect of a TFA teacher was always neutral or positive. The differences between the average TFA teacher and the average non-TFA teacher are generally not statistically significant. However, TFA teachers show less variation in quality than non-TFA teachers. The evaluation reveals the district's highest performing teachers are consistently TFA teachers, while the lowest performing teachers are consistently not TFA teachers.

The evidence in Houston indicates that TFA teachers are at the very least no worse than non-TFA teachers, and there is ample evidence suggesting they may in fact elicit greater academic gains from their students than non-TFA teachers. In addition to national and state-level approaches, some local school districts are taking matters into their own hands by developing their own alternate route programs. Elk Grove Unified School District, located in northern California, is an encouraging example. Enrolling just 18,000 students in 1987, the district now enrolls close to 50,000 and is expected to grow to 80,000 students by 2010. In order to keep up with its surging growth, the district has had to recruit teachers in unconventional ways.

Since 1993, Elk Grove has partnered with San Francisco State University to run the Teacher Education Institute (TEI), preparing teachers from noneducation backgrounds to teach in the district. While the state's typical teacher-training route can take up to two years to complete before students are able to lead their own classrooms, TEI interns take their course work during the afternoon and night for a period of 11 months, allowing them to complete a teaching practicum and serve as substitute teachers under the direction of mentor teachers and school administrators. Instruction is based on proven research-based methods and the state's academic standards. Since its inception, the program has trained 400 teachers and has a retention rate of more than 96 percent, and the performance on state tests by TEI interns exceeds those of other teachers.

The lesson for policymakers and the public is that traditional teacher-training programs do not necessarily produce graduates with superior teaching skills, while at the same time they impose significant costs and challenges on prospective teachers, especially the most talented candidates.

New Model for Teacher Preparation and Certification

There is little evidence that education school course work leads to improved student achievement. Furthermore, today's certification system discourages some of the most talented candidates from entering the profession while allowing too many poorly qualified individuals to teach. Finally, alternate routes to certification demonstrate that streamlined systems can boost the quantity of teachers while maintaining—or even improving—their quality.

The rational teacher preparation and recruitment model have the following characteristics:

1) *High Standards for Verbal Ability and Content Knowledge:* Developing challenging assessments in these areas and maintaining high passing scores would be one obvious way for states to ensure high standards for teachers. Ideally, these assessments would be linked to student academic content standards. Requiring content area majors for prospective teachers is another approach.

2) *Streamlined Certification Requirements:* Other regulations would be kept to a minimum. Attendance at schools of education would be optional; if teacher-training programmes based in schools of education proved valuable to teachers and their employers, then demand for such programs would remain. Unpaid practice teaching would not be required, and any other bureaucratic hurdles would be eliminated.

8

Teacher Preparation for Public Schools

Good teachers are the hallmark of an educational system; they are integral to children's intellectual and social development. Therefore, they must know how to teach in ways that help our children reach high levels of competence. Teacher quality is a complex phenomenon, and there is little consensus on what it is or how to measure it.

There are, however, two broad elements that characterise teacher quality: teacher preparation and qualifications, and teaching practices. The first refers to pre-service learning, teaching assignment, continued learning, and general background. The second refers to the actual quality of teaching that teachers exhibit in their classrooms. Of course, these two elements of teacher quality are not mutually exclusive; excellent teacher preparation and qualifications are expected to lead to exemplary teaching.

Perhaps the most traditional approach to characterising teacher quality is the "expert teacher study," which focuses on teachers who have been identified as successful by their administrators or peers. This field of research is rich in detail, describing how successful teachers connect what they know with how they teach. For example, researchers have found that expert teachers use knowledge about the children in their classrooms-their backgrounds, strengths, and weaknesses-to create lessons that connect new subject matter to students' experiences. They also use this knowledge to adapt their teaching to accommodate children who learn in different ways.

Expert teachers know how to recognise children experiencing difficulties, diagnose sources of problems in their learning, and identify strengths on which to build. This skill is particularly important because a growing number of students with a wider range of learning needs are entering and staying in school. One strength of the expert teacher research is that it relies on intuitive logic, which supports the belief that it is possible to identify good teachers by observing them and that, once identified, the teachers' strengths can be determined and recorded. This body of research also confirms what many people envision a high-quality teacher to be-someone who understands children and knows how to assist their learning.

Quality of Teaching Practices

The disagreement over basic skills versus complex thinking approaches to instruction is one example of the key disputes currently surrounding definitions of high-quality teaching practice. The first form of instruction traditionally has been conceptualised as the transmission of facts to students, who are seen as passive receptors. In classrooms where this type of teaching predominates, teachers typically conduct lessons through a lecture format, instruct the entire class as a unit, write notes on the chalkboard, and pass out worksheets for students to complete. In such classrooms, knowledge is presented as fact. This is the type of instruction with which most Americans are familiar.

Students then "construct" a new understanding of subject matter. Although many recent school reform efforts advocate such innovative instruction, there is much debate regarding the use and implementation of such instructional techniques. For example, opposition may come from parents and teachers who hold more traditional views of teaching and learning. Moreover, the concerns of parents, teachers, and students about access to colleges-which is based, in part, on high performance on standardised tests of recognised skills and facts-may discourage the use of innovative instructional techniques. Studies of these constructivist teaching methods have been limited because such instruction has only recently been implemented. The existing studies typically use classroom observation in a limited number of settings.

Preparation and Qualifications

Compared to other fields, disputes and ambiguities regarding the knowledge base and competence required of professionals are particularly striking in teaching . There is little dispute that teachers ought to have a post-secondary education and possess strong knowledge of the subjects they teach, but beyond this there is some disagreement about what individuals need to know and be able to do in order to teach effectively. Moreover, as researchers struggle to quantify teacher preparation and qualifications, some critics feel that studies of teachers' credentials and knowledge do not provide enough information about teacher quality-that is, indicators of teacher preparation and qualifications do not directly address the actual quality of instructional practices.

Researchers agree that understanding teacher preparation and qualifications requires more than determining whether or not a teacher has a degree or certification. In US, the National Board for Professional Teaching Standards describes teaching as a complex skill involving multiple talents. Ballou and Podgursky raise important measurement issues in their discussion of ways in which to attract "brighter" individuals into the teaching pool. They insist that flexibility in certification and personnel policies facilitates the entry of talented individuals into teaching. The implication of their argument is that extensive formal training may not necessarily create good teachers. According to their logic, extended formal training does not necessarily reflect teacher quality. It is important to note, however, the other side of the debate; that is, in addition to talent and subject-matter knowledge, prospective teachers must also be trained to teach children.

Working Conditions

In addition to teacher preparation and qualifications and teaching practice, investigations of teacher quality have included studies of what happens to teachers once they enter the workforce. This perspective stems from the premise that classrooms and schools become effective when talented people are teaching in workplaces that are stimulating and rewarding. In order to promote high-quality teaching that will in turn produce high-quality learning, teachers need support from the schools and communities in which they work and support from the parents of the children they teach.

Class size: Although the research on class size is somewhat mixed-some research studies suggest positive effects of reduced class size, others suggest little effect-it seems reasonable to assume that smaller class size may facilitate teachers' work. In order for teachers to become "experts" as defined by the expert-teacher literature, it is important for them to truly know and understand the children in their classrooms, which clearly would be easier if there were fewer children. Some of the research on class size supports this logic. For example, studies of Tennessee's Project STAR indicate that students in smaller classes significantly outperformed students in larger classes on achievement tests in mathematics and reading.

Ferguson reported similar findings in Texas; classes enrolling more than 18 students were associated with lower reading and math test scores for grades 1-7. To explain the class size effects, researchers have cited the smaller number of disruptions, the increased teacher attention for students, and the increased opportunity for student participation in smaller classrooms. Other researchers argue that reducing class size has little or no effect on student performance. In an examination of trend data from the 1950s to 1986, Tomlinson did not find a consistent relationship between class size and standardised test scores. Moreover, based on a review of the literature, Odden argued that class size reduction produces only modest gains in student achievement and does not justify the cost of implementing such reform.

Training of new teachers: Research has found that the attrition rates of new teachers are five times higher than those of their more experienced counterparts. In order to introduce beginning teachers into the profession with support and guidance, many districts have implemented formal induction programmes. These programmes can have two goals: to assist beginning teachers with instruction and to prepare them to meet state certification requirements.

A key feature of many programmes is the mentoring aspect-the pairing of an experienced teacher with a new teacher. Responsibilities of the mentor may include providing guidance on curriculum, classroom management, and assessment. It is expected that mentoring relationships play a critical role in the support, training, and retention of new teachers. Therefore, by easing the transition into full-time teaching, formal induction programmes provide new practitioners with skills and support structures to develop effective teaching practices. It is important to note that in addition to formal induction of new teachers, there are many important avenues for informal induction.

Parental support: An extensive body of research has found what many parents and educators already know-children prosper when their parents are actively involved in their education. Research has shown that support from families, including greater family involvement in children's learning, is a critical factor leading to a high-quality education. Policymakers have tapped into this important resource; for example, the National Education Goals included parental involvement in children's education as a top priority. Clearly, teachers' jobs are easier when parents work with them rather than against them. For this reason, parental support is an important feature of teachers' work environment.

Classroom Observation

Observational research has a long and growing history in the field of education. Classroom observation, as well as the collection of artifacts and information from interviews, has been employed to document teaching practices generally and to assess teaching quality specifically. Observation, as used by school systems for evaluation purposes, has been strongly criticised as having the following problems: limited competence of principals, teacher resistance and apathy, lack of uniformity within school systems, and inadequate training of evaluators. Principals often experience role conflict as they try to serve as both evaluators and instructional leaders, and they tend to lack expertise in specialised subject-matter areas, especially at the secondary school level.

Using observational data to document teaching practices is less controversial than using it to assess individual teachers for purposes of salary increase, tenure, or recertification. Observational studies, often combined with interviews or teacher logs, include investigations of teachers' pedagogical content knowledge and reasoning and the connections between education policy and teacher practices, professional development and teaching, and subject matter and curricular activity.

Observational data provide rich detail and indepth information. As such, observation is typically used to provide a detailed picture of classroom instruction in a limited number of classrooms. The Videotape Classroom Study, part of the Third International Mathematics and Science Study (TIMSS), consists of videotaped lessons in 231 eighth grade mathematics classrooms in the United States, Germany, and Japan. The report of the video study includes general findings regarding international differences in how lessons are structured and delivered, what kind of mathematics is presented, and the kinds of mathematical thinking in which students are engaged.

Teacher Testing

Standardised tests, such as the National Teacher Examinations (NTE), have been used to measure teachers' basic knowledge and skills. Teacher test scores have then been linked to student test scores. Ferguson found that teachers' scores on a test of basic literacy skills were significantly correlated with their students' test scores. Results are typically used to determine whether to grant temporary or permanent certification, and occasionally for continuation of tenured teachers. While most experts agree that having basic subject knowledge is an important prerequisite to effective teaching, critics maintain that it is not a sufficient indication of the range of knowledge and skills needed to instruct and manage groups of children. They argue that this approach does not provide a complete picture of teacher quality.

These tests only measure teachers' basic knowledge and not their pedagogical knowledge or their teaching practice. In response, organisations such as the Educational Testing Service (ETS), the Interstate New Teacher Assessment and Support Consortium, and the National Board for Professional Teaching Standards have undertaken efforts to develop new systems of teacher assessment that feature "standards-based assessments."

One example of the new generation of teacher examinations is the Professional Assessments for Beginning Teachers, the PRAXIS series, currently being developed by the Educational Testing Service as a replacement for NTE. The PRAXIS series consists of three types of assessments: (1) a computerised test of basic literacy and numeracy skills; (2) a paper-and-pencil test of subject matter knowledge and general pedagogical principles; and (3) an observational assessment of classroom teaching performance. The PRAXIS series is meant to assess potential and practices teachers at different times during their training and practice. In addition, many states have developed their own assessments as a basic prerequisite for teaching. These assessments can take the form of written tests, which may measure basic skills, subject matter or knowledge of teaching methods, and performance evaluations, which could consist of portfolio evaluation or classroom observation.

Such efforts have grown out of the recent push to identify standards for teacher and student performance. These kinds of assessments go beyond paper-and-pencil tests to include portfolio assessment and in-person testing, which incorporate pedagogy, content knowledge, and role-play/interactive sessions. Teachers may also be required to submit examples of their work through videotapes and lesson plans. Teachers are asked to analyse teaching situations and defend teaching decisions based on knowledge of subject, students, curriculum, and pedagogy.

Use of Student Achievement Tests

Many would argue that the bottom line of whether teachers are effective is whether their students are successful. The use of student achievement test score gains to assess teachers, rather than educational systems, however, has received substantial criticism. Specifically, social scientists have argued that it is very difficult to separate out the portion of student achievement gains that can be reliably attributed to an individual teacher. Numerous factors affect student achievement over the course of a school year in addition to his or her teacher: home background, student personality, attendance, school and community resources, and the peer group have all been demonstrated to affect how much students learn. In addition, critics have argued that standardised achievement tests assess minimum levels of student competence and are often limited to the kinds of knowledge that can be captured with multiple-choice

Teacher's Pre-service Learning and Teaching

Teachers' pre-service learning and teaching assignment are the first features of the teacher quality model. Aspects of pre-service learning and teaching assignment have traditionally been used to characterise teacher preparation and qualifications. Pre-service learning occurs prior to entering the classroom. Teaching assignment is investigated to determine the match between teachers' training and the main subject areas that they are assigned to teach. Growing concern that a number of the nation's teachers are underqualified to teach our children has focused attention on the quality of their pre-service learning, and especially on the institutions that prepare prospective teachers.

These institutions have been criticised for treating the education programmes as "cash cows which are conducted on a shoestring and used to fund programmes in other fields". Critics argue that schools of education should be more "intellectually solid" and more connected to elementary and secondary schools. For example, colleges and universities should improve the screening process of teacher candidates to weed out weak students, and these prospective teachers should be required to have academic majors in the fields they will eventually teach.

Finally, concern over underqualified teachers has led to increased attention toward the problem of out-of-field teaching. In order for teachers to provide the highest quality learning experiences for students, they must first understand and be able to communicate the subject matter. The number of students being taught by untrained and unprepared teachers has triggered researchers, practitioners, and others vested in education to search for solutions. Most realise that "knowledge of subject matter and of pedagogical methods do not, of course, guarantee quality teachers nor quality teaching, but they are necessary prerequisites". The lack of continuity between a teacher's training and a teacher's assignment leaves students learning from teachers that have not met those prerequisites. Researchers have debated the reasons why teachers are assigned to teach out of field. As summarised by Ingersoll, some believe that there are not enough teachers who are adequately trained in academic coursework.

Others propose that teacher unions force schools to retain older, less competent teachers and to subject new, more qualified teachers to cutbacks. Finally, some researchers believe that shortages in teacher supply force schools to hire teachers with lower qualifications. Ingersoll proposes that the low status and low pay teachers receive contributes to high turnover rates. To deal with the frequent vacancies, he argues, schools are reduced to assigning teachers to out-of-field classes. These conditions may also contribute to the number of teachers granted emergency certification.

In fact, since 1986 about 300 colleges have created extended teacher education programmes that enable students to obtain both a bachelor's degree in an academic field and a master's degree in education. In 1998, virtually all full-time public school teachers had a bachelor's degree, nearly half (45 percent) had a master's degree, and 1 percent had a doctorate. The likelihood of a teacher having a master's degree varied somewhat more years of teaching experience. This is not surprising, given that many states and districts have long required that a teacher earn a master's degree or its equivalent within a specified period of time.

Having a master's degree also varied by the concentration of poverty in the school. Teachers in schools with higher concentrations of poverty were generally less likely to hold master's degrees than were teachers in schools with low concentrations of poverty. For example, 37 percent of the teachers in the highest poverty schools had master's degrees compared with 57 percent in the lowest poverty schools. The likelihood of having a master's degree also varied by geographic region, with 60 percent of teachers in the Northeast and 51 percent of teachers in the Midwest having master's degrees, compared with 38 percent in the West and 39 percent in the South. These 1998 findings paralleled those from 1993-94, where similar patterns emerged.

Among the full-time public school teachers in the 1998 study, 38 percent had an undergraduate or graduate major in an academic field, 18 percent had a major in subject area education, 37 percent had a major in general education, and 7 percent had a major in other education fields. A higher percentage of teachers who taught at the high school level had master's degrees (55 percent) than did those teaching in middle schools (46 percent) and those teaching in elementary schools (40 percent). The likelihood of holding a master's degree increased with the number of years of teaching experience.

Thus, teachers with 3 or fewer years of teaching experience were the least likely to have a master's degree (16 percent), compared with 31 percent of teachers with 4 to 9 years of experience, 48 percent of teachers with 10 to 19 years of experience, and 62 percent of those with 20 or administration. For these analyses, each teacher was only counted once, even if he or she had more than one major or more than one degree. Major fields of study were selected in the order of academic field, subject area education, other education, and general education.

The percentages with majors in various fields varied by the instructional level of the school and years of teaching experience. While 58 percent of elementary school teachers majored in general education, 27 percent of middle school teachers and only 5 percent of high school teachers had general education majors. More high school teachers had an undergraduate or graduate major in an academic field (66 percent), compared with elementary school teachers (22 percent) and middle school teachers (44 percent). In addition, more high school and middle school teachers majored in subject area education than did elementary school teachers (9 percent).

The newest teachers were more likely to have majored in an academic field than were any of the more experienced teachers. Thus, half of the teachers with 3 or fewer years of experience had majored in an academic field, compared with 32 to 41 percent of the more experienced teachers, perhaps reflecting the recent emphasis in teacher education on majoring in an academic field rather than in education.

Status of Teacher's Certification

Teachers' certification status, the second measure of pre-service learning examined in this report, is also an indication of teachers' qualifications. In addition to requirements for formal education, teacher certification includes clinical experiences and often some type of formal testing. Most of the full-time public school teachers in 1998 were fully certified in the field of their main teaching assignment; that is, they had either a regular or standard state certificate, or an advanced professional certificate in the field in which they taught most often.

Among teachers in general elementary classrooms, 93 percent had a regular or advanced certificate, 3 percent had a provisional certificate, 2 percent a probationary certificate, 1 percent a temporary certificate, and 1 percent had an emergency certificate or waiver. Most departmentalised teachers also were fully certified in their main teaching assignment field; 92 percent indicated that they had a regular or advanced certificate in the field in which they taught the most course.

For the main teaching assignment, 4 percent of the departmentalised teachers had a provisional certificate, 2 percent had a probationary certificate, 1 percent had a temporary certificate, and 1 percent had an emergency certificate or waiver. Less than 0.5 percent of the departmentalised teachers in this study indicated that they were teaching in their main assignment field without any kind of certification. These findings on teachers' certification status essentially replicated those of the 1993-94 study. Data from both the 1998 and 1993-94 studies indicated that possessing a regular, standard, or advanced certificate was positively related to years of teaching experience. Almost all teachers in both studies who had been teaching for 10 or more years, whether in general elementary classrooms or in departmentalised settings, were fully certified in their main teaching assignment, and most of the teachers who had been teaching 4 to 9 years were also fully certified.

Teachers with 3 or fewer years of experience teaching in both general elementary classrooms and departmentalised settings, however, were much less likely to have a regular, standard, or advanced certificate than were more experienced teachers. Since some states require new teachers to start with probationary certification, all new teachers without regular certification are not necessarily less well qualified than those with regular certification. In 1998, most teachers with 3 or fewer years of experience who did not have regular certification had provisional or probationary certification. However, emergency and temporary certification was higher among teachers with 3 or fewer years of experience compared to teachers with more teaching experience.

For example, in 1998, 12 percent of general elementary classroom teachers with 3 or fewer years of experience had emergency or temporary certification, whereas less than 1 percent of general elementary classroom teachers with 10 or more years of experience had emergency or temporary certification. The results are similar for departmentalised teachers.

Teaching Assignment

Specifically, the FRSS survey measured the match between teachers' training and teaching assignment in the main assignment field-in-field versus out-of-field teaching. According to Ingersoll, one of the least recognised causes of underqualified teachers is the problem of out-of-field teaching: teachers being assigned to teach subjects that do not match their training or education. In addition, almost a quarter of all high school English teachers had neither a major nor a minor in English, literature, communications, speech, journalism, English education, or reading education. Thus, as Ingersoll concludes, a large percentage of high school students were taught by teachers without basic qualifications in the subjects they taught.

The 1998 survey and the 1993-94 survey provided data on teaching assignment and teacher education. Calculated the same way for both sets of data, a measure of in-field teaching was constructed to compare the fields in which fulltime public school teachers had undergraduate and graduate majors and minors with the fields in which they had their main teaching assignments (i.e., the field in which they reported that they taught the most courses). This measure was constructed for any teacher who taught English/language arts, foreign language, social studies/social science, mathematics, or science in a departmentalised setting in any of grades 7 through 12. Results are presented separately for grades 7 through 12 and grades 9 through 12, since there are different definitions of what constitutes secondary schooling. Because the questionnaire collected information about degrees and teaching assignments at the aggregated field level, the in-field teaching measure is also constructed at this level of aggregation.

Teachers were defined as teaching in field if they had an undergraduate or graduate major or minor in the field of their main teaching assignment. It is important to note that teachers may become qualified to teach a subject in ways that are not measured by college majors and minors. A teacher may take substantial coursework in a field without having an actual major or minor in the field. The measure of in-field teaching that is presented here differs from some of the other measures frequently seen in publications on this subject. Measures usually focus on out-of-field teaching as a measure of the mismatch between teacher assignment and teacher education.

For example, Ingersoll defined an out-of-field teacher as a teacher teaching one or more mathematics, science, social studies, or English classes without at least an undergraduate or graduate-level major or minor in the particular subject. Another approach to studying out-of-field teaching is to examine the proportion of students being taught by out-of-field teachers. In this case, Ingersoll examined the percentage of public secondary school students enrolled in 1990-91 in classes taught by teachers without at least a college minor in the field.

While examination of in-field teaching in the main teaching assignment gives a general indication of the magnitude of the match between teachers' training and teaching assignment, it does not provide the entire picture, and understates the magnitude of the problem. For example, Bobbitt and McMillen found that if the focus was restricted to main assignment field contrasted against teachers' college major or minor and certification status, then almost all teachers were qualified to teach in their main assignment field. However, if the focus was changed to include all the classes taught by each teacher, then many fewer teachers were fully qualified to teach in each class subject they were assigned to teach during the day. Thus, it is important to remember when reading the results presented below that the total magnitude of the mismatch between teacher assignment and teacher education is greater than that shown by the results for the main teaching assignment only.

In-Field Teaching in Grades 7-12

The percent of 1998 full-time public school teachers in grades 7 through 12 who reported having an undergraduate or graduate major or minor in their main teaching assignment field ranged from 82 percent of mathematics teachers to 96 percent of foreign language teachers. Comparable data from 1993-94 showed a somewhat similar distribution. The percent of the 1993-94 teachers in grades 7 through 12 who reported having an undergraduate major or minor in their main teaching assignment field ranged from 77 percent of mathematics teachers to 93 percent of the foreign language teachers. In-field teaching for the main teaching assignment in grades 7 through 12 was higher in the 1998 study than in the 1993-94 study for English and science.

A key issue in the literature on equity concerns in educational quality is the extent to which infield/ out-of-field teaching varies by certain school characteristics. Research has found that schools with factors such as a high concentration of poverty or location in an urban or central city area are more likely than more affluent or suburban schools to have higher rates of out-of-field teaching. The 1998 and 1993-94 data showed some variations in the amount of in-field teaching in the main assignment field by these characteristics. The data in tables 5 and 6 are presented differently than in other tables to allow comparisons among schools by characteristics often targeted in equity research.

Science teachers were somewhat less likely to be teaching in field in their main assignment field in schools located in central cities than in schools located in urban fringe, town, or rural areas. The 1993-94 data found that English/language arts teachers were less likely to be teaching in field for their main assignment field in schools with the highest concentration of poverty than were English teachers in schools where less than 60 percent of the students were eligible for free or reduced-price lunch. No significant differences were found by locale or percent minority enrollment in the school for 1993-94 teachers in grades 7 through 12.

In-Field Teaching in Grades 9 through 12

In-field teaching was also examined separately for teachers in grades 9 through 12, since there are different definitions of what constitutes secondary schooling. The percent of 1998 fulltime public school teachers in grades 9 through 12 who reported having a major or minor in their main teaching assignment fields was 90 percent for mathematics teachers, 94 percent for science teachers, and 96 percent for teachers of English/language arts, foreign language, and social studies/social science. Comparable 1993-94 data showed a somewhat similar distribution. The percent of 1993-94 teachers who reported having a major or minor in their main teaching assignment fields ranged from 87 percent of mathematics teachers to 93 percent of the foreign language teachers.

In-field teaching for the main assignment field in grades 9 through 12 was higher in the 1998 study than in the 1993-94 study for English, social studies, and science. In addition, for both 1998 and 1993-94, the percent of teachers who reported having an undergraduate or graduate major or minor in their main teaching assignment field was significantly lower for teachers of grades 7 through 12 than for teachers of grades 9 through 12 for mathematics, science, English/ language arts, and social studies/social sciences, indicating that teachers in grades 7 and 8 are less likely to be teaching in field than are teachers in grades 9 through 12.

Differences by poverty concentration, locale, or percent minority enrollment in the school in the prevalence of in-field teaching for main teaching assignment were not statistically significant for 1998 teachers in grades through 9 through 12. Mathematics teachers in 1993-94 were less likely to be teaching in field in their main assignment area in schools with the highest minority enrollment. No significant differences were found by locale or poverty concentration in the school for 1993-94 teachers in grades 9 through 12.

Continued Learning for Teachers

Teachers' continued learning is the second feature of teacher preparation and qualifications addressed in this report. Continued learning is particularly important because the nation's schools have been increasingly challenged by policy initiatives to "do better, and to do differently". At the core of educational reforms to raise standards, reshape curricula, and restructure the way schools operate is the call to reconceptualise the practice of teaching. American children need a broader range of skills, including higher order thinking skills and technological expertise. Teachers must learn to teach students in ways that promote such skills. At the same time, teachers face the greater challenges of rapidly increasing technological changes, greater diversity in the classroom, and a push to teach in innovative ways.

In order to meet the changing demands of their jobs, high-quality teachers must be capable and willing to continually learn and relearn their trade. This learning begins prior to entering the classroom . However, beginning teachers are often not fully prepared for the requirements of classroom teaching. Continued learning, the second aspect of teacher preparation and qualifications addressed in this report, is key to building educators' capacity for effective teaching, particularly in a profession where the demands are changing and expanding. Continued learning takes multiple forms; the two key forms are formal professional development and collaboration with other teachers.

Formal Professional Development

Some schools and school districts require teachers to participate, and certain states have passed initiatives encouraging or mandating certain types of professional development. In addition, some teachers actively seek their own opportunities for professional development. For example, college coursework completed after a teacher has started teaching is one form of professional development. However, access to professional development activities may vary widely among teachers; for example, there may be more opportunities for participation in districts located in close proximity to a university or college.

Formal professional development typically consists of school and district "staff development" programmes. Teachers often attend classes sponsored by their districts and attend workshops, conferences, and summer institutes. Workshops and conferences are the most typical form of continuing professional development. They are usually designed to meet short-term goals of implementing specific instructional change, such as the integration of technology into classroom teaching.

However, these traditional approaches to professional development have been criticised for being relatively ineffective because they are usually short term; they lack continuity through adequate follow-up and ongoing feedback from experts; they are typically isolated from the participants' classroom and school contexts; and they take a passive approach to training teachers, allowing little opportunity to learn by doing and reflecting with colleagues. A core argument is that unless professional development programmes are carefully designed and implemented to provide continuity between what teachers learn and what goes on in their classrooms and schools, these activities are not likely to produce any long-lasting effects on either teacher competence or student outcomes.

In other words, as traditionally practised, professional development activities may lack connection to the challenges teachers face in their classrooms. Because of changes in technology, in the notions of effective teaching, and in the types of students and students' needs teachers encounter in their classrooms, the survey elicited information regarding teachers' formal professional development in such areas as technology, new methods of teaching, state or district curriculum or performance standards, and accommodating students with disabilities or from diverse linguistic or cultural backgrounds. Because there is a good deal of skepticism regarding the value of formal professional development for teachers' work, the survey also requested information regarding the extent to which teachers' felt that these opportunities improved their teaching.

Content of Professional Development

In 1998, teachers were more likely to have participated in professional development activities that appear consistent with the emphasis of education reform to do things differently and better. Teachers were more likely to have participated in implementing state or district curriculum and performance standards (81 percent), integrating educational technology into the grade or subject taught (78 percent), implementing new teaching methods (77 percent), doing in-depth study in the subject area of their main teaching assignment (73 percent), and using student performance assessment techniques (67 percent) than in other areas. About half had participated in professional development in classroom management and addressing the needs of students with disabilities.

In 1993-94, teachers were most likely to have recent professional development that appears to emphasise pedagogical skills; 67 percent of teachers had professional development on methods of teaching in their subject field. Fewer teachers had any recent professional development in student assessment (55 percent), cooperative learning (53 percent), and uses of educational technology for instruction (51 percent). Teachers were least likely to participate in in-depth study in their subject field (29 percent). In addition to other issues, addressing the needs of students with limited English proficiency or from culturally diverse backgrounds has recently become a central concern mainly because of growing student populations with these backgrounds. Therefore, teacher training to meet these needs might be particularly important to schools with large minority student populations.

In 1998, teacher participation in professional development programmes that focused on limited English proficient or culturally diverse students generally increased with the percent minority enrollment in the school. For example, teachers from schools with more than 50 percent minority enrollment were much more likely than those who taught in schools with 5 percent or less minority enrollment to participate in professional development programmes on this topic (51 versus 14 percent).

Teacher Participation in Professional Development

In an era of education reform, continuing professional development is equally relevant for both new and experienced teachers as many aspects of teaching may be changing. Teacher participation in professional development may be influenced by several factors: personal motivation, school or district requirement, and state initiatives requiring or encouraging certain types of professional development. Moreover, while certain kinds of on-the-job training, such as classroom management and curriculum development, may be more relevant to the needs of new teachers than experienced teachers, those who have taught for many years may have a greater need to upgrade their skills in the use of educational technology. It is, therefore, useful to examine whether teaching experience makes a difference to participation in professional development in various content areas.

Teaching experience makes little difference to teacher participation in professional development in most of the content areas. One area in which teaching experience was, however, clearly related to teacher participation in professional development was classroom management, including student discipline. The likelihood of participating in professional development programmes that focused on classroom management generally decreased with years of teaching experience. For example, in 1998, teachers with 3 or fewer years experience were more likely than more experienced teachers to participate in such a programme, and those with 4 to 9 years experience were more likely to do so than those who taught for 10 or more years.

In some other areas, teacher participation in professional development differed between the least experienced teachers and those who were very experienced. For example, in 1998, teachers with 3 or fewer years of experience were more likely than those who had taught for 20 or more years to participate in programmes that addressed new methods of teaching (82 versus 73 percent). Newer teachers were also more likely than very experienced teachers to have participated in professional development on indepth study in the subject area of the main teaching assignment (77 versus 67 percent).

Moreover, most experienced teachers (20 or more years) were less likely than all others to participate in professional development addressing the needs of limited English proficient or culturally diverse students. The 1993-94 data on participation in professional development about teaching methods in the teachers' subject field also showed a difference between the least and most experienced teachers.

Lack of Intensity in Professional Development

A major criticism of professional development programmes is the lack of intensity and follow-up in traditional staff development programmes such as workshops and seminars. The core issue is that these programmes are typically too short term to allow for meaningful change in teaching performance. The 1998 data indicate that participation in professional development programmes typically lasted from 1 to 8 hours, or the equivalent of 1 day or less of training. The content area for which teachers were most likely to spend more than a day of professional development was in-depth study in the subject area of the main teaching assignment. However, although teachers typically need extended time to pursue research on in-depth studies, slightly more than half of teachers spent more than a day in professional training in this content area.

Since the rationale behind professional programmes is to provide the forum for teachers to upgrade their knowledge, skills, and practices, it is useful to assess the extent to which participation in these activities helped teachers to achieve these objectives. To gauge the perceived impact of professional development programmes, the 1998 survey asked teachers to assess the extent to which their participation in programmes in a particular content area improved their teaching. Of those teachers who participated in programmes in a particular area, the extent to which they believed it improved their teaching "a lot" ranged from 28 percent for in-depth study to 12 percent for implementing state or district curriculum and performance standards.

Few teachers indicated that a programme did not help at all. For every programme, 70 to 80 percent of the teachers reported that it was moderately or somewhat effective. For example, for the programme that ranked highest in its perceived impact, 70 percent of teachers believed that participation improved their teaching moderately (44 percent) or somewhat (26 percent). Teachers' perceptions about how much participation in various professional development programmes improved their teaching were examined against years of teaching experience. For most of the 1998 content areas, teaching experience was not related to teachers' perception that participation in that content area improved their teaching "a lot." The one area in which teaching experience clearly was related was classroom management.

Newer teachers were more likely than more experienced teachers to report that professional development in classroom management improved their teaching "a lot". A criticism of short-term professional development programmes is that they fail to bring about more long-term change in teachers' competencies for classroom teaching. To further assess the impact of professional development programmes, the 1998 data were explored to examine whether the amount of time spent in professional development activities made a difference to perceived teaching improvement.

The number of hours teachers participated in professional development programmes was related to how much they believed it improved their classroom teaching. For every content area, teachers who participated for more than 8 hours believed it improved their teaching more than teachers who participated for 8 hours or less. For example, teachers who spent more than 8 hours in professional development on new methods of teaching in the classroom were more likely than those who spent 1 to 8 hours to report that participation in the programme improved their teaching "a lot" (39 versus 12 percent). These patterns suggest that increased time spent in professional development is associated with the perception of significant improvements in teaching.

Relation with other Teachers

Unlike traditional professional development activities, peer collaboration has been heralded by teachers, researchers, and policymakers as essential to teachers' continuous learning. Initiatives to improve the quality and efficacy of continued learning emphasise the development of learning communities within and across schools and highlight the importance of these mechanisms to foster teacher learning. Opportunities for collaboration include those that are provided within the school and those that occur within professional networks across schools and other institutional structures.

Teacher participation in school-based activities is likely to produce positive and long-lasting change because such activities provide the basis for transformative learning. Such collaboration revolves around joint work and teacher networks. Joint work such as team teaching, mentoring, and formally planned meetings are important mechanisms for productive exchange of ideas and reflection about practice. For instance, the focus on specific subject matter and teaching strategies helps teachers to improve their content knowledge and pedagogical skills.

Mentoring is an effective mechanism for one-to-one professional guidance and for cultivating a teaching culture in which expert teachers serve as an essential resource for new teachers. All of these teaching-related activities are consistent with the view of professional development as a lifelong, inquiry-based collegial process rooted in the development of schools as collaborative workplaces.

Collaborative relationships may extend beyond classrooms and school buildings to school university collaborations or partnerships, teacher to-teacher and school-to-school networks, and participation in district, regional, or national task forces. These communities can be organised across subject matter, pedagogical issues, and significant school reforms. These networks can be powerful learning tools to engage professionals in collective work and allow teachers to go beyond their own classrooms and schools to engage in professional discourse about their own experiences and the experiences of others.

Participation in Collaborative Activities

About 60 percent of the teachers had participated in common planning periods for team teachers and networking with teachers outside the school, and about half reported involvement in individual or collaborative research. Mentoring can be an important way for teachers to share information and experiences about teaching in a one-on-one relationship. Such relationships may be particularly useful to new teachers as they seek to develop effective teaching practices. The study found that about a quarter of the teachers indicated that they had mentored another teacher in a formal relationship in the last 12 months, and 19 percent said that they had been mentored by another teacher in such a relationship.

The relatively low levels of teacher participation in mentoring reflect a pattern in which newer teachers were more likely than more experienced teachers to be mentored. The likelihood of mentoring and of being mentored by another teacher varied substantially by years of teaching experience. Teachers with 3 or fewer years of teaching experience were the most likely to have been mentored by another teacher in the last 12 months and the least likely to have acted in the role of mentor to another teacher. In fact, almost three out of five new teachers had been mentored by another teacher in the last year, suggesting that schools and/or teachers recognise the importance of such relationships early in a teacher's career.

Teachers were also asked how frequently they had participated in the activities, within a range of at least once a week to a few times a year; survey results showed considerable variation on this dimension. Among teachers who reported engaging in a particular activity, they participated the most frequently in common planning periods for team teachers, with 60 percent participating at least once a week. This was followed by mentoring another teacher in a formal relationship (42 percent) and engaging in regularly scheduled collaboration with other teachers (34 percent). While many teachers (61 percent) indicated that they had participated in networking with other teachers outside the school, the frequency of this kind of activity was low; 60 percent of these teachers reported such interactions only a few times a year.

Effect of Participation

Teachers who reported participating in an activity were also asked to indicate the extent to which they believed the activity improved their classroom teaching. In general, participation in most activities was perceived to improve classroom teaching moderately or somewhat; few teachers believed that participation in a particular activity did not help their teaching at al. Moreover, 40 percent of teachers who had a common planning period for team teachers believed that this opportunity improved their classroom teaching a lot, while one-third reported experiencing similar benefits from individual or collaborative research, or from being mentored by another teacher.

Being mentored by another teacher was not only a more frequent occurrence for beginning teachers, but it was generally perceived to be of more benefit to their teaching as well. Among teachers who had been mentored in the last 12 months, 45 percent with 3 or fewer years of experience believed it improved their teaching "a lot," compared with 18 percent of teachers with 20 or more years of teaching experience.

9

Teacher Training for Kindergarten Maths

Recent studies have suggested that teachers exert a significant influence on student learning. In particular, studies with elementary school students using value-added modeling approaches report that the overall effects of teachers may be large. If the findings of large teacher effects are accurate, they suggest that efforts to improve education for all students must seek to identify the characteristics that distinguish effective from ineffective teachers.

Becoming an Effective Teachers

Studies that have examined available indicators of teacher preparation or quality-such as academic ability, certification status, subject-matter expertise, and experience-offer mixed findings, suggesting that there is not yet a consensus as to what characteristics influence achievement. Hawk, Coble, and Swanson found that for secondary school students, mathematics achievement was positively associated with having a teacher who was fully certified in mathematics.

Fetler found a negative correlation at the school level between mathematics scores and the percentage of teachers with emergency credentials.

In an analysis using individual student data, however, Goldhaber and Brewer found that the performance of high school students on standardised mathematics and science tests did not differ according to whether their teachers held standard or emergency credentials. They found, however, that students of teachers who were uncertified or who held a private school certification in mathematics had somewhat lower achievement levels than students of teachers with a standard, probationary, or emergency certification. Rowan, Correnti, and Miller found no effect of certification status on achievement growth at the elementary level.

One caveat to be applied to studies dealing with teaching credentials is that the credential is not a standard measure of preparation, because requirements vary widely from state to state. Thus, the type of credential a teacher holds is a somewhat imperfect measure of pre-service training. With regard to subject-matter preparation, Monk, in a study of secondary high school students that controlled for prior test scores, found a positive effect of teacher coursework in both college mathematics and mathematics pedagogy on mathematics test scores. Goldhaber and Brewer found a weak positive association between high school achievement gains in mathematics and teachers with a master's degree in mathematics versus those without a master's degree or a mathematics-related bachelor's degree.

A recent study focusing on elementary school students found no significant evidence of an impact of advanced degrees on achievement gains. With regard to teaching experience, Fetler found a positive relationship between the average number of years of teaching experience of mathematics teachers and high school mathematics scores at the school level. Rowan, Correnti, and Miller found a positive relationship between teaching experience and growth in mathematics achievement for students as they progressed from third to sixth grade. Murnane and Phillips, in a study of the achievement of Black inner-city elementary school students that controlled for prior-year test scores, found a nonlinear relationship between achievement and teaching experience.

For students in grades three, four, and six, having teachers with 15 or more years of experience was positively associated with gains. For fourth- and sixth-grade students, having teachers with 7 or fewer years of experience was also positively associated with gains. For students in the third grade, having teachers with 8 to 14 years of experience was negatively associated with gains.

Instructional Practices and Student Achievement

Early childhood reading researchers recommend that attention be given in every primary-grade classroom to a wide array of early reading skills including the alphabetic principle, reading sight words, reading words by mapping speech sounds to parts of words, achieving fluency, and comprehension. In kindergarten, Ball and Blachman found that children who received instruction in phonemic segmentation and letter-sound combinations had higher reading and spelling scores than children who did not receive such instruction. While there is general agreement on the skills that should be taught, approaches on how best to teach reading are often debated.

Some research with primary-grade children has shown that no single approach to teaching reading is superior to the rest, but that balanced or integrated early literacy instruction (i.e., instruction that includes an emphasis on both phonetics and meaning) is more effective in learning to read. Certain teaching strategies and methods have also been found to be associated with greater gains in early mathematics learning. A meta-analysis of studies including kindergarten research found that the use of concrete materials or manipulatives, compared with more abstract instruction, was related to improved achievement and attitudes toward mathematics, especially during initial exposure to a skill. Also, problem-solving activities and opportunities to practice what is learned have been shown to contribute to learning mathematics concepts and skills in the first years of school.

The measurement of instructional practices, however, is less straightforward. Most studies that examine classroom practices and the links between these practices and achievement have relied exclusively, or primarily, on teacher self-reports of the frequency with which teachers use specific practices such as cooperative learning groups, inquiry-based activities, manipulatives, and open-ended assessment techniques. Several of the studies that have used this method of measuring practices have examined links between student achievement and teacher-reported use of practices that emphasise problem solving and inquiry. These practices are often called "reform based" or "standards based" and include such activities as cooperative learning groups, student-led discussions, and open-ended assessment techniques that are intended to promote the development of complex cognitive skills and processes.

Cohen and Hill's study of teacher-reported use of reform-based practices found that frequency of use was positively related to mathematics test scores among fourth-graders. D'Agostino found that in first and second grades, teacher-directed basic skill orientation was associated with greater reading and mathematics achievement, while in fourth grade, a combination of basic skill instruction and student-centered advanced skill activities was associated with greater mathematics achievement.

Several studies have attempted to examine whether the relationship between achievement and reform-based practices is different from the relationship between achievement and more traditional forms of instruction, such as the use of textbooks, lectures, and multiple-choice tests. Most of the differences in the relationships between student achievement and each of these types of practice have been found to be small. The small magnitudes of observed relationships may be attributable in part to measurement problems. Limited evidence exists regarding the extent to which survey-based measures of practices accurately capture what teachers do in the classroom.

Mayer reports results of a study that compared information obtained from survey responses to information collected from classroom observations of middle school and high school algebra teachers. Results from his study indicated that a composite of teachers' emphasis on reform-based mathematics teaching practices based on survey data was strongly correlated with a parallel composite based on classroom observations of the teachers' mathematics instruction. He found that the survey data could be used to distinguish teachers who engaged in low levels of reform-based practices from those who relied heavily on such practices, but his study also suggested that survey results masked potentially important differences among teachers in how they implemented various practices.

However, Mayer noted that when composites of individual teacher practice variables from one-time teacher surveys were grouped together to describe teachers' pedagogical style, the reliability of the resulting composites was quite high. As a result of these measurement issues, the observed weak effects between instructional practices and achievement may result from superficial implementation by teachers rather than from the practices' ineffectiveness. In addition, the kinds of instructional practices measured by most surveys constitute only a small part of the classroom instructional environment. Other aspects, such as the specific curriculum materials used and the pacing of instruction, are often not measured.

Despite the limitations of paper-and-pencil frequency-based measures of practice, they currently provide one of the best sources of information about the distributions of instructional practices used by teachers across the nation. Surveys provide a cost-effective and reliable method for gathering data on practices across different state and district contexts. Most of the existing research on practices has focused on teachers at the higher elementary and secondary grades. Because of the growing recognition of the importance of developing literacy and quantitative skills from the earliest grades, there is a need to extend the work on instructional practices to include kindergarten and other early elementary grade levels.

ECLS-K data on the instructional approaches used by kindergarten teachers permit this type of exploration. Xue and Meisels used these data to examine several classroom-level predictors of reading achievement and found that teachers' reported use of a phonics-based approach, in particular, was related to achievement in reading. ECLS-K data provide detailed information on a nationally representative sample of 22,000 children enrolled in approximately 1,000 kindergarten programs, both public and private, in the United States during the 1998-99 school year. This study uses five categories of data: achievement assessments, student characteristics, teacher qualifications, instructional practices, and school characteristics.

Achievement assessments

Assessments that included cognitive, psychomotor, and physical components were conducted with the sampled kindergarten children through one-on-one tests administered by trained individuals both at the beginning and at the end of the school year. Having both fall and spring measures is one of the features that distinguishes ECLS-K data from other longitudinal study data and makes them uniquely suited for an investigation of teacher effects over the course of the kindergarten year. The full achievement assessment used a computer-assisted personal interview (CAPI) and took approximately 50-70 minutes to complete. It included tests of reading, mathematics, and general knowledge. The test was untimed and required children to respond verbally or through pointing; no writing was required. Each test was conducted using a two-stage design, known as adaptive testing. The first stage consisted of a routing section that was administered to all students, and the second stage consisted of one of several alternative forms, the choice of which depended on (i.e., was adapted to) the child's performance on the first stage.

The reading and mathematics assessments had low-, middle-, and high-difficulty second-stage adaptive options. The purpose of this adaptive design was to maximise accuracy of measurement and minimise administration time. The content of the reading and mathematics assessments was selected to represent cognitive skills that are typically taught in kindergarten and that are thought to be important for the development of later proficiency. The reading test consisted of items measuring basic skills, vocabulary, and comprehension. The mathematics test covered five content strands: number sense, properties, and operations; measurement; geometry and spatial sense; data analysis, statistics, and probability; and patterns, functions, and algebra. Items tapping all five content strands are included in the kindergarten assessment, although the first strand is most heavily represented. Examples of the types of skills involved in this strand at the kindergarten level include counting sets of objects and solving simple addition problems using pictures.

Examples of skills included in the measurement strand include comparing the length of two objects and identifying the value of different coins. Examples of skills in the geometry and spatial sense strand include naming simple shapes and identifying lines of symmetry. Skills in the data analysis, statistics, and probability strand include reading information from a bar graph. Examples of skills in the patterns, functions, and algebra strand in the kindergarten assessment include recognising and extending patterns and sequences.

Efforts were made to include children who spoke a language other than English in the assessments. Prior to administering the assessments, a language-screening test-the Oral Language Development Scale (OLDS)-was administered to those children identified from their school records as coming from homes in which the primary language spoken was not English. Children whose performance exceeded an established cut score on the OLDS received the full English direct assessment in both reading and mathematics.

Those who did not pass the OLDS were not given the reading assessment. Students who did not pass the OLDS but who spoke Spanish were given a translated form of the mathematics assessment. Thus, the size of the sample of children who took the mathematics assessment was larger than that of children who took the reading assessment. Various methods were used to confirm that the psychometric properties of the Spanish mathematics assessment were comparable to those of the English version.

Children's Item Response Theory (IRT) scale score values are a reflection of the number of items they would have answered correctly on the assessment if they had been administered all items in the battery. The IRT scale scores may be used to calculate longitudinal measures of gains because the scores from each round of data collection are set on a common scale. From the IRT scores, gain scores were created to represent the change in relative achievement of the child over the course of the kindergarten year. All student-level models controlled for the time lapse between fall and spring test administrations, since not all children were assessed on the same day.

Student characteristics

Approximately 18,950 parent interviews were completed. Parents reported the race, ethnicity, age, and sex of each child and indicated whether the child was repeating kindergarten in the 1998-99 school year. Parents also provided information about their household income, the mother's educational attainment and occupation, and the father's educational attainment and occupation.

Teacher qualifications

With regard to certification, ECLS-K data include information about the type of teaching certificate teachers reported they possessed. These categories were chosen on the basis of the distribution of certifications among teachers given that the vast majority of kindergarten teachers in the sample were certified and few teachers fell into the alternatively credentialed or noncertified categories.

One of the difficulties inherent in research on national samples is the state-specific nature of many education programs and policies. It is important to note here that requirements for teacher certification often differ by state. Paths for attaining each type of certification vary across states in a number of respects, including the standards for admission into certification programs and the amount of in-classroom experience required. ECLS-K data also include teacher-reported information on the area in which teachers are certified. The nature of early childhood and elementary certification is particularly variable across states, and it is common for teachers to possess both.

Instructional practices

The items address a wide range of instructional practices that may occur in classrooms in the early grades, not just practices considered to be developmentally appropriate for kindergarten. Both the mathematics and reading practice items were selected to be aligned with the skills tested by ECLS-K achievement assessments. Many of the ECLS-K instructional practice items are similar in content to other research that uses teacher questionnaires to collect data on instructional practices in kindergarten classrooms.

As a result of the factor analyses, seven scales were derived for reading and six scales were derived for mathematics. The seven reading scales were phonics; reading and writing skills; reading and writing activities; didactic instruction; comprehension; student-centered instruction; and mixed-achievement grouping. The phonics scale includes items addressing teachers' emphasis on activities such as learning and practicing letters and the importance teachers place on skills such as matching letters to sounds and recognising letters.

The reading and writing skills scale measures teachers' reported emphasis on promoting students' ability to read fluently and to write using standard conventions. The reading and writing activities scale focuses on specific activities in which students engage to promote reading and writing ability, including reading aloud and writing in journals. Didactic instruction includes three items that appear to measure more traditional language arts instructional activities that students probably do as seatwork-reading from basal texts, working in workbooks or on worksheets, and writing words from dictation to improve spelling. Comprehension covers skills involved in understanding what is read. Student-centered instruction appears to address activities in which students are responsible for producing something and sharing it with the class.

The final scale, mixed-achievement grouping, consists of two items that assess the frequency of mixed achievement grouping and peer tutoring. Internal consistency reliability for the seven reading practices scales ranged from .69 to .83, with two exceptions. The reliability of the three-item didactic instruction scale was .50, and the reliability of the two-item mixed-achievement grouping scale was .48.

The six mathematics instructional practice scales were numbers and geometry; advanced numbers and operations; traditional practices and computation; student-centered mathematics instruction; mixed-achievement grouping; and measurement and advanced topics. Some of the scales focused on particular content, whereas others related more to the structure of classroom instruction. The first scale, numbers and geometry, consists of 11 items, 3 of which address classroom activities designed to promote understanding of numbers, operations, and geometry. The other eight items in this scale address instructional objectives related to numbers and geometry. The second scale, advanced numbers and operations, contains five items from the "skills" item set. In contrast to the first scale, these items emphasise skills related to somewhat advanced numeracy concepts.

Traditional practices and computation appears to identify teachers who take a fairly didactic, teacher-directed approach to instruction and who emphasise computational facility. It includes the use of worksheets, textbooks, and problems on the chalkboard and emphasises computational skills such as adding and subtracting single-digit numbers. The fourth scale, student-centered mathematics instruction, is similar to the corresponding scale identified for reading, and consists of six items that emphasise having students take an active role in their own learning.

The fifth scale, mixed-achievement grouping, consists of two items: use of mixed-achievement groups and peer tutoring. Finally, measurement and advanced topics includes one item from the "activities" set-work with rulers, measuring cups, spoons, or other measuring instruments-and eight "skills" items emphasising topics other than the basic numbers and geometry topics addressed by the first and second scales. These include fractions, data collection, probability, and estimation, along with measurement-specific skills such as "using measuring instruments accurately." Internal consistency reliability for the six mathematics practices scales ranged from .73 to .83, with one exception. The reliability of the two-item mixed-achievement grouping scale was .56.

After identifying satisfactory factor solutions in reading and mathematics, scales for each teacher were created to represent the resulting set of factors. A number of methods may be used to combine information from a set of items into a single scale. The most common method for combining items that use Likert scales is to add the scores on the individual items, a process that is typically referred to as summative scoring. When the resulting scales are based on a factor analysis, a common approach is to identify the factor on which each item has its highest loading and include that item in the calculation of a score for that factor.

Instructional Practice Scale Regressions

The instructional practice scales were based on the frequency with which teachers reported performing the instructional practices identified in the items that composed each scale.

Teacher-Level Variables: Teaching reading for 90 minutes or more per day was positively associated with the emphasis teachers placed on each of the reading instructional practice scales, with effect sizes ranging from 0.13 to 0.35. This was to be expected since the scales were constructed on the basis of teacher reports of the frequency with which they used certain practices. In addition, and possibly for related reasons, the full-day kindergarten indicator was also positive in all of the reading scale regressions except those relating to phonics and comprehension (effect sizes range from 0.16 to 0.32).

Coursework in methods of teaching reading was associated with several of the instructional practice scales, with effect sizes ranging from 0.33 to 0.66. Teachers who reported taking two, three, five, or six or more courses in pedagogy related to reading reported placing a greater emphasis on mixed-achievement grouping than teachers who did not take any reading methods coursework. Taking four or six or more such courses was also associated with a greater emphasis on student-centered instruction than taking no reading methods coursework. Taking six or more courses was associated with a greater emphasis on phonics and reading and writing activities compared with no coursework. The amount of reading methods coursework was not related to the frequency with which teachers used didactic, comprehension, and reading and writing skills activities.

Certification and possession of a master's degree were unrelated to teachers' emphases on any of the instructional practice scales. Kindergarten teaching experience was negatively associated with the reported use of student-centered instruction (effect size of -0.09). Part-time status was negatively related to the emphasis placed on phonics, didactic instruction, comprehension, and reading and writing activities (effect sizes range from -0.23 to -0.52).

School-Level Variables: School-level characteristics played a role in several reading instructional practice-scale regressions, although the relationships varied depending upon the scale. Teachers in private schools reported less emphasis on phonics, comprehension, reading and writing activities, and mixed-achievement grouping than public school teachers (effect sizes range from -0.26 to -0.63) and greater emphasis on didactic instruction (effect size of 0.49). Rural teachers reported greater emphasis than urban teachers on a didactic approach (effect size of 0.31) but less emphasis on comprehension, reading and writing activities, reading and writing skills, and student-centered instruction (effect sizes range from -0.22 to -0.41).

Suburban teachers reported less emphasis than urban teachers on student-centered instruction. School size was unrelated to all scales except phonics, in which teachers in schools with 500-749 students reported a greater emphasis than those in schools with fewer than 150 students (effect size of 0.44). The percentage of minority students was positively associated with the frequency of instruction on the phonics, didactic, and reading and writing skills scales, with effect sizes of 0.42, 0.51, and 0.50, respectively. The percentage of free-lunch-eligible students was negatively associated with the frequency of instruction on the reading and writing activities scale (effect size of -0.34).

10

Teaching Teacher Training in Health Sector

Teachers are often the main adults other than family members with whom young people interact on a daily basis. In an era of HIV/AIDS, teachers play an even more critical role of being a source of accurate information and a person with whom young people can raise sensitive and complicated issues about sexuality. As the AIDS epidemic spreads, the need becomes more urgent for teachers to discuss AIDS in the context of human development, sexuality, and pregnancy prevention.

Teachers also need to know how to protect their own health and the importance of not putting any of their students at risk through their own behaviours. Ideally, as trusted gatekeepers of information, teachers can be instrumental in imparting knowledge and skills to young people. Teachers can function as role models, advocates for healthy school environments, guides for students in need of services, resources for accurate information, mentors, and effective instructors. But to meet these expectations in the AIDS era, teachers need skills and knowledge as well as support from the educational system and broader community.

Sexuality and reproductive health (RH)/HIV education are often controversial because some individuals believe that talking about sexuality in schools may increase sexual activity. However, according to two exhaustive reviews of studies by the World Health Organisation (WHO) and the U.S. National Campaign to Prevent Teen Pregnancy, sexuality education programmes do not lead to an increase in sexual activity among young people. Even more encouraging, the reviews found that effective RH/HIV education in schools can result in delaying first intercourse or, if young people are already sexually active, increasing use of contraception.

The analysis of 250 evaluations of U.S. sexuality education programmes identified one of the key elements that led to greater behaviour change to be a teaching approach that actively involves students, is skill-based, and uses real-life situations. A recent analysis of 11 school-based HIV prevention programmes for African youth also identified teacher training as critical. "If a programme is to be faithfully implemented, teachers must be properly trained for and committed to it," the analysis concluded.

The HIV/AIDS epidemic in developing countries has resulted in more attention to developing student curricula and training teachers to use the curricula. "All ministries of education are implementing one or more interventions to combat the epidemic in the education system," reported the Association for the Development of Education in Africa in a 2001 review of regional programmes. "There is need for policies and programmes to impart requisite skills so that teachers may feel confident to teach about HIV/AIDS and issues of sexuality."

Ideally, teacher training supported by nongovernmental organisations (NGOs) or international organisations would be linked to governments from the national to the local level. Working with the appropriate governmental agencies can help ensure that activities are coordinated across programmes and that messages are acceptable and consistent. Government support and commitment can help the sustainability of teacher training so that such training is less dependent on donor funding and guidance.

Teacher Training for RH/HIV

The ultimate goal of teacher training for RH/HIV is to improve students' knowledge, attitudes, and behaviours regarding reproductive health and HIV. But effective training first has to have an impact on the teachers themselves, helping them examine their own attitudes toward sexuality and behaviours regarding HIV prevention, understand the content they are teaching, learn participatory teaching skills, and gain confidence to discuss sensitive and controversial topics.

Increasingly, countries are beginning to offer RH/HIV education in schools for younger youth (i.e., ages 8 to 12). Some teachers will need to know how to relate to students of different ages and use different materials and strategies. In addition, meeting the needs of students requires an ability to relate to young people, build trust in the classroom, and be a good listener. No subject requires better communication skills with students than teaching about sexuality, reproductive health, and HIV/AIDS.

Teacher training in the context of RH/HIV often challenges existing norms for educational institutions and the community. As communities take a greater interest in the topic, some may want to include only limited information, for example, eliminating any discussions of condoms from a curriculum. Sexuality education may not be considered as important as reading or mathematics, and given the usual limitations on resources and time, it may be the first subject to be reduced or eliminated from a school curricula. Reproductive health material is not usually on examinations because the content is often taught as part of an after-school club or is not part of the national curriculum, leading teachers to spend less time on it compared to those subjects on which their students will be tested. Teachers need preparation, skills, and support in dealing with all of these issues.

Teachers may need to work within the community in order to facilitate their work in the classroom. During the 1980s, for example, "with a group of friends, we would go to a church service and ask the priest for ten minutes to talk about HIV/AIDS," says Jane Mulemwa, now deputy chairperson of the Ugandan Education Service Commission. "We would do the same with doctors and nurses. Once the community is more open, it is easier in the classroom." Teachers also need skills in dealing with management issues in school systems and local schools.

For example, teachers and schools may need to go beyond structured classroom settings and work with local NGOs on such issues as orphans and school fees. "Our thinking is trapped in the box of the conventional concept of a school being a supplementary institution, which presupposes that the pupils come from stable and secure homes that provide them with general care and support," says Professor Wally Morrow, South Africa Ministerial Committee on Teacher Education. Conditions are far different in many countries, especially those in Southern and East Africa with high HIV prevalence, where orphans and others may not be able to attend traditional schools.

Involving the community in pre-service teacher training can also be helpful. Ultimately, teacher training should not be viewed in isolation from the larger community. David Mbetse, a geography teacher in South Africa, attended training in sexuality education over the objection of the head of the school. He then taught the subject to his pupils, whose parents reported him to the head of the school for non-Christian behaviour. "From then on, I had to go and talk to people within the community to explain what this training was for and to sensitise them to HIV/AIDS," he says. He subsequently managed to convince the head of the school to have some people living with AIDS talk to the pupils and to establish support groups.

Materials to assist teachers with these multiple tasks and to supplement formal teacher training curricula are beginning to emerge. For example, WHO together with Education International, a membership group of nearly 300 national unions of teachers and workers in education, produced a manual emphasising how teacher training fits into the broader framework of teachers' lives. The manual can be used in training workshops to help teachers gain skills to reduce HIV infection among themselves, skills to strengthen their ability to advocate and build support for effective RH/HIV prevention in schools, and skills in teaching developmentally appropriate curricula for young people.

Impacts of Sex Education for Teachers

Although reviews of sexuality education programmes have emphasised the importance of teacher training, little research has addressed issues such as which type of training works best, how long the training should last, and how to involve the community in training. The topic of teacher training can include not only the training itself but also what types of people receive the training, the degree of support for teachers by the school system and community, and the issue of teachers covering only certain aspects of a curriculum (e.g., omitting controversial segments).

Research has found that teacher training can positively affect teacher attitudes toward sexuality education and participatory techniques. In Thailand, 35 teachers received training that emphasised a better understanding of young people and their environment, the teachers' own attitudes and values toward HIV/AIDS and sexuality, and learning and practising key skills in facilitating HIV/AIDS and sexuality training. Using pre- and post-tests and interviews, researchers found that following the training, the teachers had more knowledge and understanding of HIV/AIDS, more positive attitudes toward young people's sexuality and toward people living with HIV/AIDS, an increased willingness to use participatory methods, stronger facilitation skills, increased communication and better relationships with students, and a greater commitment toward teaching about sexuality and HIV/AIDS.

Some research has shown that teacher training incorporated into a broader school district intervention can influence students' behaviours. A project in the Soroti district of Uganda with students ages 13 to 14 included teacher training on RH/HIV in the existing structures of the school district, using a health educator, the local teacher training college, and other resources. Two years after the baseline survey, students whose teachers had received the training reported a significant decline the training reported a significant decline both in having sexual intercourse in the past month and in the average number of sexual partners. The control group did not have similar reductions.

Research points to several factors beyond teacher training itself that affect the impact on students. A project in rural Masaka, Uganda, provided five days of training to teachers, adapting portions of an AIDS prevention curriculum e-time was too short. Also, teachers did not address some of the major HIV/AIDS prevention issues due to fear of community disapproval and controversy and lack of supportive guidance. The research team recommended that the programme be integrated into the national curriculum and that teachers be trained in participatory methods while still in teacher training college.

In Jamaica, teachers who were trained in using experiential teaching methods, participatory exercises, roleplays, and the performing arts were more likely to use those methods in their classrooms than those without the training. However, changes in behaviour in the students were not significantly different from those students not exposed to the new curriculum. Researchers attribute the lack of change at least partially to the fact that the intervention was implemented for only one semester of the school year. Other reasons included the lack of supplies, lack of administrative support, not enough monitoring of the teachers, and few refresher courses.

A recent UNICEF review of projects in East and Southern African concluded that life skills programmes that addressed HIV/AIDS issues are more effective when teachers explore their own attitudes and values, establish a positive personal value system, and nurture an open, positive classroom climate. Programmes appear to be more effective when teachers use a positive approach emphasising awareness of values, assertiveness, relationship skills, decision-making, real-life situations, and self-esteem.

In the 1960s, population education programmes sought to create awareness about the relationship between the benefits of smaller family size and national development. Family life education (FLE) or life planning skills education programmes included parts of population education and added decision-making, family issues, and parental responsibilities. Few FLE programmes, however, included sexuality and reproductive health information, such as sexual behaviour and contraception. The few attempts to provide sexuality education in schools were seldom implemented, and when tried, controversy often led to their demise.

As the AIDS epidemic moved into the general population, many African countries embraced the need for a more formal education process to teach youth about HIV/AIDS, including, in some cases, broader issues of sexuality. A study by the Population Council in Kenya, for example, found that a large majority of primary and secondary school teachers, as well as parents and guardians, approve of the teaching of adolescent growth and development, including topics such as STIs and AIDS, family and gender roles, reproductive physiology, and puberty and menstruation. Support is weakest for teaching sexuality and family planning—though even family planning, the least popular subject, is supported by about 40 percent of primary teachers and parents. About 80 percent of secondary school teachers approve of teaching family planning in secondary schools.

While the HIV/AIDS crisis has resulted in new attention to sexuality education in schools, Africa's educational system is struggling to adapt meaningful education tools. Inadequate funding and poor infrastructure plague education systems throughout sub-Saharan Africa. Teachers overwhelmingly report a shortage of teaching materials, and available materials are often outdated. In many countries a shortage of teachers has resulted in younger, less-experienced teachers who have not had training in teaching RH/HIV issues.

Increasing the emphasis on RH/HIV education in pre-service training programmes is a cost-effective place to start and can go to scale through the mandates of ministries of education, reaching even remote areas within countries. While pre-service training offers an excellent opportunity to shape the thinking and style of teachers before they enter the profession, RH/HIV is not always covered at this level of training. So efforts at the pre-service level should be increased.

Meanwhile, in-service training programmes for those already teaching are taking place in some countries, often sponsored by international organisations or local NGOs. Sometimes these initiatives are supported by the government and linked to its ministry of education. In other cases, they function as separate activities and lack sustainability. In-service training programmes can vary from a few hours to several weeks.

Policies and Practices

All youth need information on abstinence and delayed sexual initiation as well as RH/HIV issues. Sexually active young people may need RH/HIV services such as STI treatment, condoms, other contraceptives, or voluntary counselling and testing for HIV. An important prerequisite to school-based programmes themselves, and subsequently effective teacher training, are clear policies and guidelines supporting young peoples' access to both information and services. These policies should be widely known by teachers and service providers and should be implemented.

In a survey by Education International of its member teacher unions, 84 percent of those responding, most of them in Africa, said they received little or no support from reinforcing policies on the prevention of HIV/AIDS and related discrimination. Where supportive policies have not been adopted, administrators at the local level may have to cope with input from religious groups and other stakeholders who may object to aspects of a curriculum, particularly discussions about condom use for those already sexually active.

Without clear guidance from mandated policies, teachers may avoid controversial areas. Evaluations of teacher training programmes show that teachers frequently fail to teach topics in which they have been trained because they feel uncomfortable with the subject, they are inadequately trained, or they lack materials. A review of 11 African school-based HIV prevention programmes identified selective teaching as a problem, especially regarding controversial areas such as condom use. An in-depth analysis of how an HIV/AIDS curriculum was taught in western Kenya by Action Aid, a United Kingdom-based group, found that some teachers select which messages to give, choose not to teach HIV at all, or rely "solely on messages on abstinence.... Sexually active youths will not only feel excluded from messages forbidding premarital sex, but will also have limited access to potentially life-saving information."

To change policies and social norms, policymakers need to consider the factors that deter teachers from discussing controversial areas, including the influence of religious institutions, the fear of being fired, teachers' personal beliefs, and a general belief that discussions about condoms will encourage promiscuity. Clear policies and procedures, careful selection of teachers for training, ongoing training and support, and frequent teacher monitoring and supervision are required to minimise this problem.

When courses are not mandated nationwide, teacher training may be less uniform and more unpredictable. "Some reproductive health training in guidance and counselling courses cover more theory and concept rather than real situations with youth," says Joy Mukaire, former Ugandan country representative for the U.S.-based Pathfinder International. A teacher training programme in Uganda includes training about sexuality in a course on "Christian Religion and Ethics," which emphasises Christian approaches to marriage, dating, relationships, human sexuality, homosexuality, drug abuse, and other subjects, with less detail on contraceptive methods, including condom use.

Debates exist about whether RH/HIV training should be a separate course or integrated into the general curriculum. The recent UNICEF review of life skills programmes in Africa found that placing education about STIs and HIV within the context of personal development, health, and living skills often works better than integrating the material into other subjects where it may get lost.

Policies in Africa are not clear on how long the teacher training needs to be, the role of refresher courses, and needs for supervision and monitoring. A review of teacher training in Nigeria and Cameroon emphasised that developing expertise in sexuality education takes training, practice, feedback, supervision, refresher training, and time. Also, refresher training solidifies and reinforces the gains made during initial training. When one trained teacher repeated the same basic training course after an interval of two years of teaching, she remarked that she learned more from the second course than from the first because now she knew exactly what she needed to know.

HIV-related Attrition

The HIV/AIDS-related attrition of teachers and managers in African educational systems is alarming. Mortality, morbidity, and absenteeism in high-prevalence countries are expected to increase rapidly over the next 10 to 15 years. The World Bank estimates that in Kenya, Zambia, and Zimbabwe, about 1.5 percent of the teaching profession is lost each year to AIDS, and that the percentage of teachers who are HIV-positive is more than 30 percent in Uganda and Malawi, 20 percent in Zambia, and 12 percent in South Africa.

Teacher attrition due to HIV/AIDS leads to deteriorating educational systems through stress on the human-resource base, worsening ratios of educators to students, loss of experienced teachers, increased demands on staff health benefits, and pressure on educator training colleges to keep pace with the demand for new teachers.

The United Nations, as part of its Millennium Development Goals, seeks to achieve "education for all" by 2015. This goal seriously strains the capacity of many educational systems in Africa to produce adequate numbers of trained teachers, says Bradford Strickland, senior education advisor at the U. S. Agency for International Development (USAID) Africa Bureau. "The strain on human resources from HIV-related illnesses and death makes it even harder to correct existing shortages. In Zambia, for instance, the Ministry of Education trains 2,000 teachers each year, while annual losses from all mortality average around 1,000 per year. Attrition from other causes still has to be added to the losses from mortality."

Sexual Harassment of Students

A growing body of research has documented the problem of sexual harassment of students by teachers. In one Ugandan district, 31 percent of schoolgirls and 15 percent of schoolboys reported having been sexually abused, primarily by teachers. Students stated that they generally knew which teachers were involved in sexual relationships or engaged in other inappropriate sexual behaviours. Thus, these teachers would have no credibility with students when teaching RH/HIV content. Many communities remain silent on this issue, either feeling pressured not to respond or feeling helpless to do anything about it.

The most common pattern is sexual relationships between male teachers and female students, which reflects traditional gender-based power differentials and patterns of cross-generational sex. In such situations, the female student will be the one who has to deal with a pregnancy resulting from this sexual exploitation and will likely have to quit school. Attitudes of teachers are often shaped by a culture that promotes gender inequity or sexual harassment. However, past experiences can be overcome. A project in South Africa revealed that after receiving training, teachers were less likely to support gender-based violence and felt confident to discuss this issue in the classroom. Of the teachers who received training, 47 percent were women who had previously experienced physical abuse from a partner, while 25 percent were male teachers who previously reported that they had been physically abusive to a partner.

The South Africa project used both a "train the trainers model" and a "whole school" model. The "train the trainers" model educated two representatives from each of the selected schools and relied on these representatives to relay the training to others. The "whole school" model trained all school employees, including the administration and the cleaning staff. While both approaches led to significant changes in teachers' perceptions about the role of school in addressing gender-based violence, the "whole school" model resulted in a greater commitment from school management.

TEACHER TRAINING PROJECTS

A review of teacher training and curriculum design activities in 16 countries in sub-Saharan Africa revealed various stages of development. Below are short summaries of activities in Malawi, Mozambique, and Nigeria, followed by longer discussions of teacher training projects in Ghana, Kenya, Uganda, and Zimbabwe. In Malawi, USAID, UNICEF, and the Ministry of Education are developing a preservice training curriculum for use in the seven teacher training colleges in that country, adapting a life skills curriculum developed by UNICEF. At the same time UNICEF, the Swedish International Development Agency (SIDA), and UNFPA are developing an in-service curriculum for primary school teachers in standards 5 to 8.

In Mozambique, the Ministry of Education is revising its 1996 teacher training curriculum and has developed a strategy to train teachers in the new curriculum in all 410 teacher training centers in the country, both pre- and in-service.

In Nigeria, guidelines for comprehensive sexuality education have been developed, using international guidelines developed by the Sexuality Information and Education Council of the United States (SIECUS). The Association for Reproductive and Family Health is training teachers in Oyo State to teach reproductive health in secondary schools.

A project called Strengthening HIV/AIDS Partnerships in Education (SHAPE) has included teacher training as a key component of its efforts to improve HIV/AIDS education in schools. SHAPE is using a curriculum called "Window of Hope" to train teachers in HIV/AIDS issues at teacher training colleges. Sponsored by the Ministry of Education and USAID/Ghana, SHAPE is being implemented by World Education.

In 2003, the project conducted baseline research with teachers at 10 of the 41 teacher training colleges to gain understanding of the future teachers' HIV/AIDS knowledge, attitudes, and practices. A total of 1,752 teacher trainees were randomly selected to complete the questionnaire, and qualitative data were obtained from 80 trainees who participated in eight focus groups. The findings will be compared to data gathered after the implementation of the Window of Hope curriculum at the colleges. As part of the larger effort, the project also conducted a two-day sensitisation session on HIV/AIDS for the tutors, those who teach the curriculum to the trainees.

Findings indicate that myths regarding HIV transmission and prevention exist and that many trainees do not consistently practice HIV prevention in their own lives. Almost all trainees acknowledged that they are at risk of HIV infection. The majority of trainees knew of at least one situation when a student was having a sexual relationship with a teacher. The analysis of the assessment found that "education is needed specifically in the areas of myths of transmission, use of consistent prevention methods, stigma of people living with AIDS, student/

teacher abuse, and confidence in discussing HIV-related issues with students."

Late in 2003 and early in 2004, SHAPE and the Ministry of Education conducted monitoring and support visits to 37 of the 41 teacher training colleges. The visits sought to ensure that the Window of Hope training curriculum was being delivered properly and effectively, including the use of participatory facilitation techniques, experiential activities with supportive materials and exercises, and the proper amount of time. The monitoring found both positive and more challenging developments.

Among the positive findings were that some colleges have established relationships with local NGOs and community groups to supplement the curriculum and the work of the tutors. Younger tutors have embraced the experiential nature of the curriculum, but the older tutors tend to rely on traditional lectures and didactic methods. Some colleges have already added AIDS prevention clubs, which provide training for students wanting to be peer educators.

Challenging findings included the fact that some colleges lack the resources needed for all of the exercises, including flip charts, VCRs, and photocopiers. A lack of clarity existed in some colleges about whether the curriculum is to be integrated into other subjects or taught separately.

In six rural communities in western Kenya, from 1999 to 2003, a project targeting youth ages 10 to 19 sought to build the capacity of teachers to teach sexuality education. The effort was coordinated by the Population Council in collaboration with the Programme for Appropriate Technology in Health (PATH) and the Kenyan ministries of education, health and gender, sports, and culture as part of a larger operations research project.

About 100 teachers from primary and secondary schools were trained in content and participatory methods. Teams comprised of three teachers and the headmaster from 33 schools, including five secondary and 28 primary schools, attended the trainings. Guidance and counselling staff were also trained to provide counselling, and each school was required to provide a designated room for counselling. Refresher courses were offered once a year, and bimonthly meetings were held for teachers on thematic areas using other technical experts. Each theme was also the area of focus for the teachers' work with students for that quarter.

Each student was supposed to receive 12 to 33 hours of instruction in units of one to two hours, with the longer time preferable to allow for greater interaction with students. The curriculum was originally developed by PATH and included a full range of RH and HIV topics. In most schools, the RH/HIV content was taught as an extra-curricular activity, although all students were expected to participate. Each school had its own arrangements for when the course was offered. Some offered it during physical education class, some on weekends, and others during lunch.

Religious leaders approached the project, asking to become involved. Consequently, about 80 of these leaders were trained in adolescent health and sexuality. Since many of the schools had a religious affiliation, agreement had to be reached on the curriculum content. As a result, issues like condom use and homosexuality were not included in the intervention, although the teachers still were expected to teach issues related to HIV/AIDS and other sexually transmitted infections.

Ministry of Education supervisors provided monitoring and support for the teachers once per term using a monitoring checklist. These supervisors were trained in supportive supervision and were provided with additional skills to offer technical assistance should problems arise. More difficult problems were referred to the project's field coordinator. The project did not analyse changes in teacher methodologies or attitudes as a result of the project but instead focused on knowledge, attitudes, and behaviours with students, who received other community interventions as well.

Teachers are the most reliable source of information for youth ages 10 to 14 and that the project promoted more openness and willingness to discuss issues at all levels of the community. In addition, while the project was underway, the Kenyan government mandated that schools provide students with information on HIV/AIDS. Teachers in the school intervention areas reported that their training in the life skills curriculum enhanced their ability to carry out this mandate.

In the early 1990s, as part of a multisectoral, highly publicised AIDS prevention programme endorsed by the president of Uganda, the Uganda AIDS Commission developed a National Operational Plan that emphasised abstinence, delayed sexual debut, and mutual faithfulness as the highest priority strategies for youth ages 11 to 20. The use of condoms was considered a secondary strategy. Efforts to train teachers to teach sexuality education operated in that context, with data indicating that substantial increases in abstinence among youth did occur where teachers were trained.

From 1994 to 1996, the African Medical and Research Foundation (AMREF) coordinated a school-based project in 95 primary schools in the Soroti district in northeastern Uganda, which has an overall population of about 450,000. The students were in their final year of primary school and had an average age of 14. The project trained about 5,900 head teachers, science teachers, senior women teachers, senior men teachers, peer educators, tutors, and final year students of the teachers colleges. Each of the schools established a four-person core project team that mobilised other teachers so that all were involved in project activities.

Senior women tutors and male science teachers received one week of training in sexuality-related content. Senior women and men tutors were designated by the schools to give advice to students. Senior teachers were responsible for counselling and answering day-to-day questions while other teachers taught the content. Local leaders and headmasters received a one-day training to sensitise them to the project.

The project had one full-time health educator and otherwise relied on the existing staff in the district. The project used a life skills curriculum developed by PATH and supplemental materials adapted from other sources. Trained teachers were supervised quarterly using a checklist, which was sent to AMREF and then to the district education system if there were problems. Support to teachers was also provided through five- or six-day annual refresher training courses held during the December/January holidays.

The project worked through existing school structures including meetings of parents and school health committees, and through community resources such as district steering committees, technical staff, and district administrators for various governmental departments. School health clubs and trained peer educators helped develop activities such as songs, dramas, and poems related to HIV/AIDS. In addition, upper primary school students mentored lower primary students. Schools also had question-and answer boxes, and questions were answered weekly or bimonthly during health parades or group sessions.

A study of the first two-year intervention in the Soroti District of Uganda found that teachers were the main source of information for youth. Among students in the sample from the intervention schools, the percentage that stated they had been sexually active fell from 43 percent in 1994 (123 of 287) to 11 percent in 1996 (31 of 280), while no significant change was reported in a control group. The Soroti project continued to collect data through 2001, when a post-intervention report found further declines in sexual activity. Those in the intervention group reported increased communication and sharing of information among the pupils themselves, and between the pupils, their teachers, and their parents.

A postintervention study showed that 98 percent of the girls were not sexually active in 2001, compared to 94 percent in 1996 and 66 percent in 1994, according to Dr. Francis Oriokot, senior health advisor for AMREF/Uganda. Reported pregnancies leading to school dropouts fell from an average of three per year per school down to none in about 70 percent of the schools. Teachers reported that the training helped them to improve lesson planning and teach and structure activities better.

In another effort in Uganda, UNICEF is working in 31 school districts, focusing on adolescent development, life skills, and sexual and reproductive health. Teacher training centers help teachers to communicate with adolescents using participatory methodologies and youth involvement approaches adapted from UNICEF's guide, "Talking with Adolescents." The tutors at the training centers are attached to the Ministry of Education and provide ongoing support for 10 to 20 schools in an area. The project has other components, including the establishment of school and facility-based youth-friendly services so young people can be referred for counselling and clinical services. No evaluation of this project is yet available.

These teacher training efforts in Uganda suggest that primary schools are viable entry points for health education; that mainstreaming HIV/AIDS information into the broader school health programme facilitates a more free discussion of HIV among children and teachers, with less stigma than a separate course on HIV/AIDS; and that community involvement contributes to the success of a teacher training and sexuality education effort.

In Zimbabwe, a mandatory AIDS education curriculum has been integrated into related subject areas in all primary and secondary schools. More than 6,000 schools are now teaching the prescribed curriculum. All national, regional, and district education officers have received training through the programme, along with more than 2,000 teachers, who have been trained in AIDS education materials as well as participatory methods. Some 5,000 trainees have begun similar training in teacher training colleges. This successful training system began on a national scale in the mid-1990s. The Ministry of Education and Culture and UNICEF coordinated the effort, which included both in-service and pre-service training for teachers.

The in-service programme used a cascade model, training trainers at the national level who then trained other trainers at the next level, and so on through five stages until the local-level teachers were finally reached. The model could, in theory, reach the 35,000 teachers involved in AIDS education. The pre-service component included the introduction of AIDS education curriculum into the 27 tertiary colleges under the Ministry of Higher Education in 1994. An evaluation of the project found that it underestimated the challenges involved in an in-service training programme that relied on five stages of cascading down to the local level. It suffered from turnover of trainee teachers and lack of links between the in-service and pre-service efforts, such as coordination of materials.

The evaluation concluded that teacher training needs detailed planning and careful monitoring. "Participatory methods should be integrated into the whole training through the use of hands-on participatory training for teachers, with live teaching sessions with children," the analysis concluded. "A close link should exist between in-service training and pre-service training, and between training and materials."

Selecting Good Teachers

All school staff should receive at least an orientation to a new RH/HIV programme so that they have accurate information for themselves and their students. Those teaching the RH/HIV curriculum itself need more extensive training and should be selected from among those motivated to teach RH/HIV. Not all teachers are interested in, capable of, or well suited to teach sexuality content to adolescents—selecting the right people to teach RH/HIV curricula is challenging. Teachers may not want to teach this topic because of their own issues related to sexuality, their personal beliefs, religious or community pressures and controversies, or concerns about their own HIV status.

Adding RH/HIV content is often viewed as a burden to an already crowded curriculum. Since financial resources are scarce, teachers must be motivated in other ways such as involving them in planning and facilitation, offering continuing education credits or certification, or acknowledging their efforts publicly. Those who want to teach the subject will bring their energy and dedication to the task and likely be more effective.

Teachers who provide RH/HIV education need to have a capacity for "health literacy"—the capacity to obtain, interpret, and understand basic health information and services and the competence to use this information to enhance the learning of concepts and skills by students, parents, and staff. Without this capacity and an ability to deal with the subject matter and with youth, teachers may be ineffective and lack confidence.

In one study in Kenya, both parents and students reported higher levels of confidence in teacher competence than teachers had themselves. Only 21 percent of parents and 14 percent of students felt that teachers did not have sufficient knowledge to teach about HIV, compared to 45 percent of the teachers. Teachers of RH/HIV content also need to be approachable to students and have a healthy rapport and comfort level for difficult and sensitive questions.

Teacher Training Curricula

In developing and using teacher training curricula for RH/HIV, programme managers, curriculum developers, education officials, and others should be aware of four key aspects of the curriculum: goals and guiding principles, teacher-focused content, methodology and facilitation skills, and management and structure. A teacher training curriculum for RH/HIV should be based on clearly stated goals and guiding principles. It should include the rationale for teaching RH/HIV to youth and the values, beliefs, and practices the curriculum is designed to promote. The content of the curriculum, ideally, should naturally flow from its goals and principles.

Six goals in training teachers in RH/HIV are to:

— Provide accurate information about human sexuality

— Develop effective classroom skills

— Advise on teaching materials and methods

— Develop personal comfort with reproductive and sexual health issues

— Develop competence in reproductive and sexual health language

— Provide information on school and community policies

Guiding principles in a teacher training curriculum may vary depending on the sensitivities of the government and NGOs involved. Some principles embraced by NGOs may not be consistent with policies of other sectors, such as religious organisations or governments. Principles for a teacher training curriculum could include the following:

Youth and Sexuality

— Youth can make good decisions when provided with complete information and skills.

— Young people have a right to information and services.

— Individuals and society benefit when youth are able to discuss sexuality with their parents, teachers, and other trusted adults.

— Sexuality is natural and a life-long part of being human.

— Young people should be encouraged to abstain from sexual intercourse as the only sure protection against unplanned pregnancy and STIs, but they should also be taught about contraceptives, including the use of latex condoms, for those who are or will become sexually active.

Teachers and Sexuality

— Teachers are more effective in communicating sexuality information when they have reflected upon their own attitudes, feelings, beliefs, experiences, and behaviours regarding sexuality and how these affect their ability to communicate.

— Experiential learning is an important way to facilitate increased knowledge and changes in behaviour.

Human Rights and Sexuality

— Every person has dignity and worth and should be free from discrimination based on gender, race, age, ethnicity, religion, culture, sexual orientation, or HIV status.

— No pressure, force, or coercion of any kind should be used to get people to participate sexual activity against their will or to exploit them in any way.

— Culture, tradition, and religion serve as important cornerstones in the development of an individual, and their positive influence should be acknowledged, respected, and utilised.

— Young people have a right to privacy and confidentiality.

— People with HIV deserve compassion and support.

Because teachers in training are adults, adultlearning theories should be incorporated throughout the curriculum, such as building on existing knowledge and experiences of participants. In addition, clear learning objectives should be included to help teachers understand the changes in knowledge, attitudes, skills, and behaviours expected of them.

Teacher-Focused Content

The content of the teacher training curriculum can be divided into four general areas: personal feelings and attitudes, knowledge, skills, and other issues. Personal feelings about sexuality and attitudes toward young people are critical. The curriculum needs to engage teachers in examining their own experiences, biases, and judgments about youth and sexuality and raise their level of tolerance and comfort in discussing sensitive issues.

The curriculum should help teachers to assess their own risk of HIV infection and encourage them to learn their own HIV status. This process gives teachers a greater investment in the issue and hence a greater commitment to helping youth. "Training must first and foremost enable teachers to protect themselves and train themselves before they can effectively train children in prevention," reported the Education International survey in Africa.

The curriculum should provide teachers with basic reproductive health knowledge, including information related to the transmission, diagnosis, and treatment of STIs and HIV/AIDS. Teachers should be able to explain clearly the dangers arising from STIs and HIV, provide basic information about the infections, and give clear instructions about the actions needed to prevent STIs or treat them effectively. Basic information on pregnancy prevention, the fertile period during the menstrual cycle, and contraception is also needed. Ideally, teachers would also receive information on sexual expression and orientation, although this area remains controversial.

Training should also help teachers understand a broader range of adolescent behavioural and psychosocial development issues, so they can assist students with problem-solving, critical thinking, interpersonal relationships, empathy, and the ability to cope with stress. Teachers need to learn new skills to teach RH/HIV, including conflict management and negotiation skills for RH/HIV issues, critical for teaching young people problem-solving and decision-making skills.

Teachers need to learn assertiveness skills as well so they can model them for students. "How can teachers teach a topic like assertiveness when they themselves are not assertive and when teachers and society do not value assertiveness?" asks Jacqueline Nshemereikwe, a university lecturer in Uganda. Curriculum content might also include other elements such as how RH/HIV could be presented to various ages, religions, and ethnic groups. The different needs of boys and girls require special emphasis, along with the cultural and gender dynamics with which males and females must cope.

Curricula and class exercises may need to differ by gender and in some settings, boys and girls may need to be taught separately. Attention should be given to social and cultural factors that influence RH/HIV and to assessing and meeting the needs of youth, including those with special needs or living in special circumstances. Ideally, teachers would learn about the different types of RH/HIV curricula that could be taught in primary and secondary schools.

Development of Facilitation Skills

The training curriculum needs to cover the methodology, techniques, approaches, and activities best suited to teaching sexuality content to young people. The curriculum ideally would model participatory and experiential teaching techniques so that teachers will use those techniques with students. The development of facilitation skills requires both instruction and opportunities to practice them.

Participatory teaching methods cover a wide range that include: brainstorming, group facilitation, use of media (newsprint, videos, etc.), role-plays, case studies, debates or structured discussions, games, exercises, and visual and performing arts (singing, dancing, drama, and drawing). For such methods to work, teachers need to learn how to develop visual aids and other materials, how to integrate student content into lesson planning with participatory methods, and how to create a coherent classroom environment that is conducive for learning.

In a review of lessons learned from life-skillsbased education for preventing HIV risks, UNICEF found that a range of teaching and learning methods have helped to improve knowledge, attitudes, skills, and risk behaviours. WHO has developed a briefing kit for teachers on STIs that offers various participatory techniques that go beyond providing basic information. Through participatory methods, teachers can impart valuable skills to their students, such as negotiation skills, communication skills, and other techniques that young people can use to negotiate their way through sexual situations and to avoid risky situations.

Teacher training should prepare teachers for the challenges of using participatory methodologies, such as working with large classes in restricted spaces, coping with teaching environment that may seem more chaotic than a lecture format, and building the confidence to cope with student questions that they may not be able to answer. Many teachers are accustomed to didactic styles of teaching and come from cultures where young people do not question adults or interact with them openly. The training methodology needs to provide opportunities to practice their skills, use their knowledge, and examine their attitudes and values, just as students will have to do.

A project by WHO and UNESCO trained tutors and 100 primary and 32 secondary school teachers in using participatory methods. The evaluation of its impact a year later found that teachers did not feel confident to carry out experiential learning activities such as role-plays and reverted to more conventional teaching methods. Teacher training on participatory methods can be supplemented by the involvement of local NGOs and community groups with appropriate skills and services. This might include presentations by the staff of health facilities, youth-serving organisations, theater and drama groups, and peer educators.

Management Issues

The curriculum should include information on the structure of the school environment, resources available within the school and community, and established policies that will affect the teachers. Other overall management issues in the curriculum could include:

— Leadership, management, and coordinating mechanisms for programme delivery

— National and local policies

— School policies and procedures for handling sensitive issues

— Guidance on other sources of information, available community-based services for student referral, and links to these resources

— Roles and responsibilities of key players

— Sufficient time for teachers to master new teaching methodologies

— Provision for ongoing training and support to encourage and reinforce learning through peer coaching, working with a mentor teacher, peer support groups, or in-service training

Ideally, a curriculum would include a clear plan for supportive supervision. That can provide important feedback and help teachers identify areas of weakness so they can improve their performance. Such supervision can help teachers address problems or concerns and modify teaching techniques to meet student needs. This requires time and effort but will help assure greater teacher competence.

11

Teacher Training for Democratic Teaching

Education for democratic citizenship (EDC) needs to be a feature of formal as well as informal education, and an entitlement for all citizens in a democratic society. The idea of EDC is not new. There has been an element of civic or citizenship education in various European countries for many years. In the main this has consisted largely of informing learners about the political system—that is to say, the constitution—in place in their country, using formal methods of instruction. The underlying model of citizenship has therefore been a passive and minimal one. Citizenship for the vast majority of ordinary people has consisted in little more than the expectation that they should obey the law and vote in public elections.

In recent years, however, events experienced and changes taking place across Europe have challenged this model of citizenship. They include:

— ethnic conflicts and nationalism;

— global threats and insecurity;

- development of new information and communication technologies;
- environmental problems;
- population movements;
- emergence of new forms of formerly suppressed collective identities;
- demand for increasing personal autonomy and new forms of equality;
- weakening of social cohesion and solidarity among people;
- mistrust of traditional political institutions, forms of governance and political leaders;
- increasing interconnectedness and interdependence—political, economic and cultural—regionally and internationally.

In the face of challenges such as these, it has become clear that new kinds of citizens are required: citizens that are not only informed, but also active—able to contribute to the life of their community, their country and the wider world, and take more responsibility for it.

Changing Trends in Education

Traditional models of education are simply not equipped to create the kind of active, informed and responsible citizenry that modern democracies require. In important ways, they are failing to respond to the demands of a rapidly changing social, economic, political and cultural environment—for example, by continuing to:

- — deny learners the opportunity to explore and discuss controversial social and political problems by emphasising the teaching of academic knowledge, at a time when they appear to be losing interest in traditional politics and forms of political engagement;
- — focus on fragmented disciplinary knowledge and classic 'teacher-textbook-student' learning at a time of rapid advance in new information and communication technologies;
- — restrict civic education to factual information about 'ideal' systems at a time when citizens need to be taught practical skills of participation in the democratic process themselves;
- — nurture dominant cultures and 'common' national loyalties at a time when political and legal recognition of cultural difference has come to be seen as a source of democratic capital;
- — detach education from the personal lives of learners and the interests of the local community at a time when social cohesion and solidarity is declining;
- — reinforce the traditional divide between formal and informal and non-formal education at a time when education needs to address the needs of lifelong learning;
- — promote state-focused forms of education and training at a time of increasing interconnectedness and interdependence at a regional and international level.

What is required are new forms of education that prepare learners for actual involvement in society—forms of education that are as much practical as theoretical, rooted in real life issues affecting learners and their communities, and taught through participation in school life as well as through the formal curriculum. The need to provide such teaching presents important challenges for the teaching profession. It means learning new forms of knowledge, developing new teaching methods, finding new ways of working and creating new forms of professional relationships—both with colleagues and with learners.

It emphasises teaching based on current affairs over the understanding of historical systems, critical thinking and skills teaching as well as knowledge transmission, co-operative and collaborative working rather than isolated preparation, professional autonomy instead of dependence on central diktat. It requires a change in how we perceive learning, from an idea of learning as teacher-centred to learning through experience, participation, research and sharing.

The Council of Europe launched in 1997 a comprehensive project on EDC with a threefold task: clarification of key concepts, development of teaching and learning strategies, and the establishment and monitoring of innovative learning practices in so-called 'sites of citizenship'. The project developed a new approach to EDC. It combined the idea of multi-faceted practice with 'bottom-up' strategies, was based on common European values, and aimed at active citizenship and participation through lifelong learning in a range of formal and non-formal educational settings.

The approach was influenced by the Council of Europe's Declaration and Programme on education for democratic citizenship based on the rights and responsibilities of citizens of 1999, in which it is stated that EDC should become an "essential component of all educational, training, cultural and youth policies and practices." A year later the European Ministers of Education adopted the Cracow Resolution and the draft common guidelines for education for democratic citizenship. The document re-defines democratic citizenship by adding a set of new dimensions to an earlier commonly accepted concept of citizenship and reinterprets the way it should be learned and taught.

In particular, democratic citizenship was seen as encompassing several dimensions—including the political, the legal, the social and the economic. In doing so, it ratified the notion that democratic citizenship should be seen as applying not only at the regional and national level, but also at the European and the global level. The principles and contents of EDC were further clarified in the Committee of Ministers' Recommendation Rec 12 on Education for Democratic Citizenship. The recommendation states that education for democratic citizenship should be at the heart of educational policy-making and reform, and is "fundamental to the Council of Europe's primary task of promoting a free, tolerant and just society."

As such, EDC may not be equated with a single discipline, school subject, teaching or training method, educational institution or learning setting, learning resource, group of learners or a particular period of study. It is a comprehensive and holistic approach that encompasses, in a lifelong perspective a broad range of other approaches, programmes and initiatives, formal and in-formal, as well as non-formal—such as civic and political education, human rights, intercultural and peace education, global education, education for sustainable development, etc.

Consequently, it is seen as a complex tool for advancing value-oriented knowledge, actionbased skills and change-centred competences that empower the citizens for a productive life in a pluralist democracy. In particular, EDC, promotes self-awareness, critical thinking, freedom of choice, commitment to shared values, respect for differences, constructive relations with others and peaceful conflict-resolution, as well as global perspective—all of which are important for personal development of a democratic citizen and a democratic society as a whole.

Need Effective Systems for Teacher Education

However, while the need for an active, informed and responsible citizenry is now generally agreed, and role of education in creating such a citizenry is almost universally acknowledged, current evidence suggests that there is a real gap between the rhetoric of need for EDC and what actually happens in practice. One of the main findings of the Council of Europe's All-European Study on EDC Policies was of a considerable "compliance gap", almost a gulf, in member states at all levels and sectors of education, between policy intentions for EDC and the provision of adequate resources—information, human, financial and technological—to turn those intentions into effective policies and practices in reality.

In particular, the All-European Study on EDC Policies concluded that: "despite the importance it is given in policy statements, teacher training schemes do not give enough support to EDC implementation efforts". It found, overall, that very little systematic support was provided for initial or in-service teacher professional development in EDC. In most cases, in-service teacher training activities were the result of ad hoc initiatives, school-based schemes or school-civil society collaboration. EDC initiatives in initial teacher education, where they existed, were largely generalist in nature. Seldom were there cases when EDC-related teacher training schemes were brought together under one government programme or one EDC policy implementation scheme—exceptions being the Association for Citizenship Teaching in England, the Federal Centre for Civic Education in the Russian Federation, the 'New Horizons' teacher training programme of Czech universities, and civics and citizenship studies for teacher training in Hungary.

Clearly, the success of EDC depends upon teachers. It is they who introduce and explain new concepts and values to learners, facilitate the development of new skills and competences, and create the conditions which allow them to apply these skills and competences in their everyday lives at home, in school and in the local community. However, the recognition of the role of EDC in preparing people for life as active and responsible citizens broadens teachers' responsibilities and sets them new challenges. Some of these challenges were noted as long ago as 1987 at the 15th Standing Conference of Ministers of Education of the Council of Europe meeting in Helsinki.

The Resolution on new challenges for teachers and their education draws attention to the kind of assistance and encouragement teachers need—including pre- and in-service training in which they can acquire the personal and social skills needed for new forms of classroom management, team work and co-operation with local and other partners, as well as an understanding of European values and their transmission to young learners in modern, pluralist societies. It also means training in familiarity with intercultural education, education in human rights and democratic citizenship, European and global issues, and health and safety education.

In addition, the new role for EDC also extends the categories of actors who should be involved in the promotion of EDC. Recommendation 12 on Education for Democratic Citizenship presupposes the active involvement not only of school teachers, but of a range of other actors working in non-formal and informal education—especially, trainers, advisers, mediators and facilitators. The quality of EDC therefore depends upon the preparation and training of all those involved, both prior to and during their EDC service.

The evidence suggests that, to date, attempts to deliver the kind of comprehensive, interdisciplinary and dynamic training that teachers and other actors require have only been limited and sporadic. There is, therefore, a definite need throughout the member states to develop more effective systems for delivering appropriate and co-ordinated training programmes in EDC, both at pre-service and in-service level.

Affecting Factors in the Provision of Teacher Training Programmes

Having outlined the critical role of teacher education in the implementation of EDC policy, we now consider some of the key factors affecting the provision and nature of training for teachers—although many of the issues apply equally in the case of other relevant actors. These fall roughly into two categories: factors arising out of the nature of EDC and the way in which it is developing in schools; factors arising out of the nature of teacher training as it is currently exists.

Nature of EDC in Developing Schools

The nature of EDC and the way it is currently developing in schools has important implications for the provision and nature of the teacher training that is required. They include:

EDC is both a School subject and a Whole-school Approach

It encompasses discrete subject teaching, cross-curricular work, democratic school practices and community involvement. This means that training is both an issue at a general level for all teachers, and a concern for specific subject teachers—particularly those who teach citizenship or civic education and closely related 'carrier' subjects, such as history, political science and social science. To the extent that EDC is a whole-school process, training is also an issue for school principals and senior management teams. It also suggests the need for teacher training to be carried out at several different levels, including:

— curricular content
— teaching and learning methodologies
— management skills
— people or participative skills.

Bottom-up Way of Development

Particularly in countries with decentralised education systems and high levels of teacher autonomy. Where this has happened, teacher-training activities—insofar as they exist—tend to be fragmented and unsystematic, consisting of independently organised courses, seminars or conferences delivered partly or wholly by a mixture of local and international nongovernmental organisations or intergovernmental organisations, pedagogical institutes and professional associations. This suggests the need for research into the overall level and nature of existing provision within individual member states and a more co-ordinated approach to future provision both at regional and state level.

An Innovative Concept

The democratisation of education has significant implications for schools and teachers In some circumstances it means countries having to fundamentally change their teaching orientation quite radically—especially, in education systems dominated by traditional, 'topdown' approaches to teaching and learning and hierarchical approaches to authority. The sorts of training activities that are required can often therefore be wider in scope than is usually the case in teacher training, and have to address fundamental issues relating to the development of more open, participative and democratic teaching and learning styles.

For inservice training, in particular, this may involve teachers in a considerable amount of unlearning of old and deeply ingrained teaching processes and practices. A didactic, teacherled, textbook-dominated, knowledge-based orientation has to be replaced by one emphasising student involvement, a broader range of teaching methods and a more skills-based approach.

EDC is Not Always Well Understood

There has been a tendency among some practitioners and policy-makers in some circumstances to have a restricted view about what EDC is and what it means in schools. It is not uncommon, for example, for the aims of EDC to be identified with the making of 'good' citizens, in the sense of polite and caring individuals. Understood in this way, the provision of EDC in schools becomes limited to the cultivation of caring and considerate behaviour and the creation of opportunities for students to become involved in 'good works', rather than an intellectually stimulating activity that challenges young people to engage with their status as citizens of society.

Another form of misunderstanding is to see EDC simply as a kind of teaching method without any specific content—often identified as 'discussion' in a rather general way. Yet another is to identify EDC with personal development—that is, with the nurturing and growth of self-confidence, self-esteem and so on. Where EDC has been conceived in ways like these, it has quite naturally had low status in the eyes of policy-makers and practitioners in institutions in comparison with other subjects and, consequently, been seen as a low priority for teacher training.

In providing teacher training programmes in EDC, therefore, there will in many cases be a need to address at a fundamental level the concept of EDC that teachers possess and the types of attitude—or prejudice—that accompany it. Training programmes cannot take it for granted that teachers will either understand what EDC is—at least in the sense now generally accepted at policy level throughout the member states—or regard it as being a good thing.

EDC is Implemented Differently in Different Countries

In some countries EDC is taught through a cross-curricular approach, whilst in others it may be seen as integral to one or more existing school subjects, such a social sciences, history or geography. There are countries where EDC is a regular or optional school subject, and others where there are no programmes at all. Similarly, EDC may appear under a variety of names -for example, civic education, citizenship education, human rights education, intercultural education, character education, global education. It may have different aims and emphases, or use different teaching methods. It may be related solely to formal settings, or be expanded to include informal and non-formal learning.

Training programmes need to be aware of these differences in practices and to consider the extent to which they reflect different conceptualisations of EDC and lead to differences in citizens' competences. If they do, these differences may actually hinder the promotion of a common European approach to education, and, consequently, the development of common democratic culture in Europe.

Factors that Affecting the Development of Teacher Training

There are also factors affecting the development of EDC training that come from the nature of teacher training as it currently exists.

Teacher training is delivered through a wide range of providers: They include government agencies, non-governmental and inter-governmental organisations, pedagogical institutes, professional communities, and private and commercial companies. This often makes for fragmented provision, with the result that government agencies are sometimes unaware of the level or quality of EDC training taking place nationally. It is important therefore in developing programmes of teacher training in EDC to ascertain just what different modes of delivery are available within individual member states and how these might be co-ordinated and sustained.

Primary and secondary teachers normally have access to different forms of training: Teacher training provision usually reflects the fact that primary teachers are generalists and secondary teachers are subject specialists. This makes it likely that very different forms of EDC training will be needed for primary and secondary school teachers—at both pre-service and in-service level.

Beginning and experienced teachers have very different training requirements: Pre-service and in-service training are normally structured in quite different ways, reflecting the different needs of teachers at different stages in their teaching careers. Pre-service training is generally organised or recognised by the state and provided through universities, teacher training colleges, training schools or commercial companies for a significant period of time—often for 3 or 4 years.

In-service training, on the other hand, can vary from the occasional seminar or workshop to a further university degree. This means that training geared towards pre-service training in EDC is likely to be of a different order from that provided for inservice training. In some circumstances, it may also mean that where resources are restricted a choice has to be made between support for one or the other as part of a national strategy -for example, in practice in-service courses are often better suited for training a larger number of teachers in a short time, as well as being cheaper than initial teacher training programmes.

In-service training is often voluntary: In less centralised education systems, the decision of whether to attend training seminars or embark upon a course of training is often left up to the individual teacher. Funding may or may not be made available to cover the cost—either to the individual or to the school concerned. In order to develop a more systematic approach to EDC training it is important to develop mechanisms—beyond outright compulsion—that will encourage teachers to take up opportunities for in-service training in EDC, or encourage schools to reflect more closely upon the EDC training needs of their teachers—e.g., by linking EDC training to career development, or to school improvement or development plans.

Teacher training makes increasing use of new technologies: Web-based resources are steadily being used to support teacher training—particularly at inservice level. They include case studies, information on teaching styles, exemplar lesson materials and self-evaluation tools—sometimes in the form of distance learning packages. It raises the question of how on-line resources might be best developed to provide aspects of teacher training in EDC.

Support Structures and Mechanisms for Effectiveness of Teacher Training

The effectiveness of teacher training policy depends in the first instance on the quality of the structures and mechanisms designed to support it, and of the resources that are available to deliver its objectives—information, human, financial and technological. This is as true of EDC as of any other aspect of education. However, the process of creating the structures needed to promote teacher training in EDC is as yet comparatively undeveloped in many countries—both in policy and in practice. Different countries are at different stages in this process. European countries do not all share the same educational histories and traditions, or have access to the same sorts or levels of resources required to convert EDC policy into a reality. While the development of teacher training in EDC is well under way in some countries, in others it is still only in its infancy.

Policy-making

The development of a systematic approach to EDC training begins at the level of policy. This in turn has its origins in political commitment. What is required, therefore, is a written policy explicitly expressing the desirability of a national approach to teacher training in EDC and a commitment to find the resources needed to make this a reality in practice. Ideally, it should include both pre-service and in-service training, but where resources are limited it may—in the short term at least—be restricted to the latter. It should also include a commitment to creating space for both state and non-state agents in relation to EDC training—particularly for the important role that NGOs can and do play. National policy that is based on a poor or insufficient understanding of present states of affairs in practice is unlikely to be successful. It is important, therefore, that policy development is preceded by an audit and evaluation of EDC training initiatives that are already under way in the country—as well as a current needs assessment.

Policy Implementation

It is essential that responsibility for policy implementation should be clearly identified within state agencies. Where responsibilities lie in different areas of administration—for example, responsibilities for pre- and in-service provision, it is important that these are subject to some form of overall co-ordination, e.g., through ministries, universities, pedagogical institutes, national EDC training centres or professional bodies. There is an argument, too, for having forms of regional co-ordination where conditions allow, including regional advisers.

Co-ordination at national level must not be confused with a centralised, authoritarian—or 'top-down'—approach to policy implementation, however. It is in the nature of EDC development in schools in many countries to date that the introduction of elements of EDC both into the taught curriculum and into the culture of the school have originated in grass-roots initiatives—school-based schemes and school-civil society collaborations - often supported by NGOs or encouraged by governmental 'pump-priming'.

At the same time it is in the nature of EDC as a concept that opportunities should be created for 'bottom-up' initiatives to flourish. The ultimate aim of EDC is to equip people for life in a more genuinely democratic society, and one way in which this can be achieved is through the development of a more genuinely democratic educational culture. Understood in this way, national co-ordination is not about the issuing of diktats by central government but rather the unification of sundry ad hoc EDC training initiatives in one systematic national or federal programme or policy implementation scheme. This means finding ways to support the voluntary activity of individuals, schools and local networks as well as monitoring and evaluating the quality of the provision that arises out of it.

Pre-service Training

The first step in developing EDC in pre-service training is the introduction of a general element of EDC into the training of all new teachers. At primary level this should be done in the context of the whole school curriculum, as a form of cross-curricular competency. At secondary level it is best done within the context of the trainees' specialist subjects, e.g. how EDC can be taught through social science, etc.

In each case, training should cover both EDC content and teaching methods—including how they might be applied in the teaching of other school subjects—and issues that relate to the creation of more democratic and participatory approach to school life in general. The second step is to introduce some element of specialisation into EDC training at secondary level—for example, courses in which EDC is taught jointly with another school subject, or as a teacher's 'second subject'. This will be more effective the closer the affinity between EDC and the subject in question.

In general, subjects like history, social science and political science are the most likely to provide suitable partners, but this is not to rule out other like geography or native language teaching—or religious education, where it is taught following a non-confessional, multi-faith approach. The third step is to introduce EDC as a specialist subject at secondary level—or, in the case of joint courses, to make EDC the senior partner. This may also incorporate training in how to co-ordinate EDC initiatives across a school as a whole and, ultimately, to provide a basis for training other teachers in EDC techniques. However beneficial training courses or postgraduate programmes are, for pre-service EDC training to be genuinely effective, supplementary support structures and mechanisms are likely required. They include:

School placements or specialist training schools

It is crucial to EDC pre-service training that beginning teachers are provided with opportunities to practise EDC in real settings. This means establishing a system of school placements or specialist training schools. In the case of school placements, it is important that the schools chosen exemplify good practice in EDC and are able to provide their trainees both with experience of EDC within a range of settings and with professional support. Where EDC is still emerging in schools, this may mean giving attention to the way in which schools are prepared for this responsibility—itself a training task.

Specific standards or competences

In order to guarantee quality of provision of pre-service EDC training—especially where a range of different kinds of institutions may be involved—it is useful to identify a set of EDC-specific standards or and to make the acquisition of these a qualification for entry to the teaching profession. Professional standards or competences exist at the general level in a number of countries, but as yet they have seldom been made subject-specific.

Monitoring quality

Alongside the existence of professional standards should be some means of assessing the extent to which pre-service EDC training activities are providing appropriate opportunities for these to be developed in beginning teachers. This means some system of overall quality control or assurance, or official inspection, of the institutions or organisations providing the training.

Induction period

Once the pre-service training course is over, it is helpful if new teachers are allowed a period of time in which, as they embark on their professional practice, they are able to consolidate what they have learned—say, for an initial year. Among other things, this should involve a limited teaching timetable—for example, 75 per cent or 80 per cent, and some system of professional support.

Professional support

Professional support in EDC for beginning teachers may be provided externally—for example, by institutions and organisations responsible for initial training, professional associations, government agencies or other bodies. However, it should also include within-school support. This means some system of professional mentors or tutors, i.e., practising teachers who have as part of their responsibility the role of supervising and supporting beginning teachers in their EDC work. How this role is understood depends to some extent on whether EDC is seen as a general competency expected of all teachers or a separate subject—or both.

In-service Training

The first step in developing a systematic approach to EDC training at in-service level is to audit the range of training activities that are currently taking place in a country. These are likely to be organised and delivered by a range of providing institutions, including non-governmental and inter-governmental organisations, higher education institutions, and private and commercial companies.

The second step is to begin to organise all these activities into a unified programme, deciding which to provide with active support at a national level and, where there are obvious gaps in provision, which of the gaps to begin to fill first. This is not to be confused with the kind of centralised educational programme in which every last detail is dictated by central government. Rather the idea is to bring together a range of different activities—local as well as regional—into one systematic approach, which thereby gains in effectiveness.

In terms of general strategy, a number of different ways of proceeding or areas of support are possible:

- EDC training aimed at school principals, senior managers and governors;
- general EDC training for all teachers;
- specific training aimed at developing specialist EDC teachers;
- training in EDC training aimed at developing school or locally-based EDC trainers.

In terms of method, training practice may focus either on individuals or on institutions—or both. It is important, especially in situations in which EDC training is still only in its infancy or where resources are restricted, to be able to concentrate support on grass-roots initiatives that are already under way. It is also in the spirit of EDC as a concept to support 'bottomup' forms of EDC training, e.g., local voluntary networks, communities of practice or EDC peer groups.

A community of practice is an extended group of people—not all of whom are necessarily practitioners as such—sharing a belief in and promoting the same set of educational understandings and practices. A peer group is a small, local group of practitioners who meet together to give each other support in certain aspects of their practice. In providing an effective system of EDC in-service training, a number of supplementary support structures and mechanisms are important. They include:

Training materials

Training materials for EDC in-service training can take different forms, e.g., case studies, teaching strategies, assessment techniques, model lessons, schemes of work, exemplar school activities, etc. These may be web-based, or take the form of a distance learning package or professional handbook. They may also take the form of curriculum materials -e.g., textbooks or manuals—that either have an EDC training element attached to them or are drawn up in such a way as to induct teachers into new forms of practice. Training videos are a particularly effective and economic way of disseminating good practice to a large number of teachers and schools. They also have the advantage of being able to display examples of EDC practice in real time. Training materials should reflect not only the need for teachers to be skilled in the sorts of pedagogy associated with EDC, but also in the subject content of EDC and their development as "teacher researchers".

Quality assurance

Quality assurance is a mechanism for making EDC more effective at school level. It allows schools to evaluate their achievements, audit existing levels of teacher skill and knowledge, and identify their development needs. EDC self-evaluation tools allowing teachers to audit their level of knowledge, skill and expertise now exist in some countries, and also self-evaluation tools for schools as institutions.

Accreditation and formal qualifications

Another way of supporting in-service EDC training is through the state-recognised accreditation or certification of training courses. A system of formal qualification is made all the more effective by being closely linked to teachers' personal career development and/or school development or improvement plans. The purpose of accreditation is not 'licensing' in the sense of censoring certain types of practice, as was sometimes the case in the past, but to provide an incentive for teachers to volunteer for additional training by linking competence development to financial reward and/or career development.

Specialist training and demonstration schools

Establishing a system of schools as "centres of excellence" for EDC can have the dual function of providing high quality school placements for trainee teachers following pre-service training courses and a facility for in-service training. Data on such "centers of excellence" could be displayed on the internet portals of the Ministries of Education, local Departments of Education, or via the non-formal education networks.

A professional association

A strong EDC professional association operating at a national level is able to support EDC training in many different ways—through arranging and co-ordinating courses, seminars and workshops to disseminating research and setting up local networks of practitioners. It can also act as a national focus for EDC training, through the publication of a professional journal, newsletter or e-bulletin and/ or the establishment of a national EDC centre.

International cooperation and exchange programmes for teachers

As the Council of Europe project on Education for Democratic Citizenship has demonstrated, there is a lot to gain from international exchange of good practice in teacher training for EDC. A number of recommendations for teacher training in EDC were voiced at the 2003 conference on bridging the gap between EDC Policy and Practice, and at the 2005 conference on teacher training for EDC. The following was suggested in 2003:, when discussing what should be done:

— Before starting a course, engage in discussion about democracy, rights and responsibilities, attitudes, values;

— Identify and prioritise the category of teacher to receive training. Specialist EDC teachers? Other subjects?

— Develop a historical and philosophical approach to EDC training, and not only for teachers;

— Train teachers in groups from the same school rather than individual teachers (whole school staff;

— Set up co-operative schemes: Council of Europe and teacher training institutions and NGOs to support EDC;

— Focus on how schools may be opened up to the local community;

— Conduct public discussions on the role of the teacher in society;

— Universities need to have Chairs with regard to training of teachers for EDC.

The 2005 conference on the new and roles of teachers in promoting education for democratic citizenship and human rights education provided ideas for action in member states. As it appears in the report of this conference, teachers must be sensitised to the true meaning of EDC which does not merely include teaching history and political literacy. EDC is an umbrella term encompassing class management techniques, teaching strategies, school management, assessment and feedback, learning styles, non-formal education and a host of skills, initiatives and approaches. Teachers need also to be trained to make EDC visible and audible in school and out of school. EDC needs to permeate school life, so teachers need to know how to make use of all opportunities school offers.

International cooperation can help raise awareness of best practices in Europe and support democracy learning in the years to come.

Teacher Competences

The professional competences and dispositions that teachers require in order to support students in their learning in EDC. The core objective of EDC is to encourage and support learners to become active, informed and responsible citizens. Such citizens are:

— aware of their rights and responsibilities as citizens;

— informed about the social and political world;

— concerned about welfare of others;
— articulated in their opinions and arguments;
— capable of having an influence on the world;
— active in their communities;
— responsible in how they act as citizens.

Helping students to develop as active citizens involves much more than presenting them with factual information about their country's constitution or justice system, it also involves practical and conceptual knowledge; a range of skills and aptitudes; and attitudes and values.

It is helpful to think of these as the three elements of EDC learning:

— Knowledge and understanding;
— Skills and aptitudes;
— Attitudes and values.

These three different elements are essentially interrelated. This is because democratic citizenship—while it can be the subject of academic study in its own right—is first and foremost a practical activity. It means that the different elements should be learned together, not in isolation. Teachers trained in EDC need not only to recognise the interrelationship of these three elements at each stage of a young person's education, but also to be able to see how they can be integrated in a practical way in the classroom These three elements of EDC learning apply to four dimensions of active citizenship:

— political,
— legal,

— social,

— economic.

Each dimension requires distinctive knowledge and understanding; skills and aptitudes; and attitudes and values. They enable learners, respectively, to be able to be integrated into society, to draw on the cultural tradition and developments in the countries where they live, to find work and to participate in political decision-making. The specific elements of EDC learning, integrated as they may be both in learning and in practice, can best be described separately.

Knowledge and Understanding

What one should know and understand in EDC reflects the basic structure of politics, which can be summed up in three elements: politics relies on an institutional framework, politics is essentially a process of decision-making, and politics focuses on handling complex issues on which the future of society depends:

- Understanding the institutional framework
  - Politics—how does our democratic system work?
  - Law—which bodies and institutions are involved passing laws and making decisions?
  - Economy—how is public finance organised and what is the role of business?
  - Society—how is society made up?
- Learning how to participate and engage in action
  - Citizenship—what are my legal rights and responsibilities?

- — Participation—how can I make a difference?
- — Human rights—what are our basic human rights and how are they applied in society?

— Understanding and forming an opinion on key issues

- — Current affairs—what is in the news and who selects it?
- — Interest groups—who is involved and how do they wield power?
- — Values and ideologies—what beliefs and values come into play?
- — Conflict resolution—how can disputes be resolved peacefully?
- - Globalisation—how is globalisation affecting my life and those of others abroad?
- — Sustainable development—how can this be achieved?

Skills and Aptitudes

The sorts of skills and aptitudes required in EDC teaching include:

- — Expression—how to express and justify a personal opinion;
- — Critical thinking and argumentation—how to make judgements and form arguments;
- — Problem-solving—how to identify and define EDC problems and arrive at common conclusions;
- — Decision-making—how to negotiate collective decisions;

— Intercultural skills—how to see issues from other people's points of view;

— Research—how to investigate and present EDC issues;

— Political action—how to engage in forms of lobbying and campaigning;

— Evaluation—how to reflect on personal and collective learning.

Attitudes, Values and Dispositions

Knowledge and skills are tools that can be put to any use. They do not of themselves lead to the practice of active and responsible citizenship. Taken to the extreme, knowledge and skills in democratic citizenship will not only help democrats, but can be turned into weapons to destroy democracy. What is also required is the desire to participate positively in society, and the will to make this desire a reality. This shows how EDC learning always must include a normative, value-based dimension. The essence of democratic attitudes and values is that democratic citizenship should not only be understood and made use of, but cherished and appreciated and, if necessary, defended against scepticism and autocracy. However, while it is perfectly legitimate for values and attitudes of this kind to be encouraged in schools, they should not—unlike knowledge and skills—be assessed formally.

— *Attitudes and dispositions for democratic citizenship*

  — Openness;

  — Respect for cultural and social differences;

  — Readiness to share and delegate;

  - Trust and honesty;
  - Commitment to truth;
  - Respect for self and others;
  - Tolerance of ambiguity and open, undecided situations;
  - Assertiveness—putting forward my opinions clearly and with courage;
  - Democratic leadership—including others in decision-making;
  - Teamwork and co-operation.
- *Values for democratic citizenship*
  - Human Rights;
  - Equality;
  - Freedom;
  - Justice;
  - Peace;
  - Interdependence;
  - Pluralism;
  - Sustainable development.

Required Competences in Support EDC

The competences that teachers require in order to support EDC should be coherent with active and responsible citizenship. They fall into a number of general categories:

Subject knowledge

In the first instance, teachers require sound subject

knowledge—that is, of the aims and purposes of EDC, and the range of knowledge and understanding, skills and aptitudes, and values and dispositions that are to be developed in young people. Without this kind of knowledge the teacher is unable to select learning objectives and plan activities to achieve them, or to achieve a balance between knowledge, skills and values learning.

Curriculum content

Teachers also require a reasonable knowledge of curriculum content, i.e., social, cultural, political and economic understanding—in relation to their own country and to the world as a whole. This will be expected to include understanding of the institutional framework of democracy, the constitution, and human and civil rights.

Teaching methods

While background knowledge and subject knowledge equip teachers with what is to be taught in EDC, these do not by themselves tell teachers how EDC is to be taught. Developing the right sorts of teaching methods, and learning how and when to use them, is one of the most important areas of teacher training in EDC.

Management and people skills

As EDC is a whole-school approach as much as it is a classroom subject, teachers also need to develop important EDC-related management and people skills—for example, in how to make links with and involve the local community, how to encourage student participation in school life, how to deal with potentially controversial and sensitive subject-matter and so on.

Reflection and improvement

EDC is dynamic as it is based on what happens in society and on individuals' relations to their community and society at large. This characteristic requires the capacity to reflect on and improve EDC regularly through teachers' personal and professional development and training, as well as their involvement and contribution to quality assurance of EDC within the whole school. Professional competences of this kind take time to develop and are built up through practice. It is unreasonable to expect all of them to be perfectly achieved before a teacher begins to teach EDC.

Personal Qualities

In addition to professional competences, there are certain personal qualities that are needed by teachers of EDC in their day-to-day dealings with students. While none of these qualities are specific to EDC as such, they are more central in EDC than in other subjects and essential if teaching and learning in EDC is to be effective. They include:

— fairness—dealing justly with students

— openness—willing to listen to and learn from students

— impartiality—-valuing student contributions equally

— empathy—seeing issues from a student perspective

— assertiveness—challenging prejudice and aggressive behaviour

— sensitivity—treading carefully with controversial and emotive issues

— respect—recognising cultural and social differences

— authenticity—being willing to share own views when appropriate

— self-awareness—owning up to own prejudices

— commitment to dialogue—encouraging discussion and debate.

It is also important that teacher interest in issues relating to democratic citizenship and human rights should not be restricted to the professional activity of teaching, but extend beyond the classroom into everyday life. In this way students are helped to see that EDC is not an abstract activity but relates to real-life issues in the world today. Emphasis on qualities and interests of this nature reflects the need for teachers to be ambassadors for the values of active and responsible citizenship and transmit them through their relations with students and the ethos of the life of the institution. While some of these are a matter of temperament or character and not generally amenable to change, others may be enhanced through training—and, to that extent, have a role to play in EDC training programmes.

Teaching Methods

As teaching methods in EDC are perhaps less well understood than its content. As in every other teaching and learning activity, there is a cycle:

— *Plan*—select EDC learning objectives taking account of students' prior learning in EDC and design learning activities in order to achieve these objectives;

— *Implement*—carry out the learning activities;

— *Assess*—check to see whether students have learned what it was intended they should learn;

— *Evaluate*—reflect on the success of the overall learning activity and plan subsequent teaching accordingly.

Each of the stages of this cycle demands a particular repertoire of skills from the EDC teacher. These are not simply generic skills that apply in every subject, however. Teachers of EDC need, for example, to learn the sorts of learning activities that can be used in EDC—e.g., discussion, role play, simulations, project work—and how they can be used effectively in EDC. Similarly, they need an understanding of the kinds of learning that can be assessed in EDC, and how they can be assessed. EDC is a distinctive form of educational activity that aims to equip young people to participate as active citizens, and as such employs distinctive forms of learning. Teachers need to be fluent in these forms of learning and able to put them into practice in different settings. They include forms of learning which are:

— *Inductive*—presenting learners with concrete problems to resolve or make a decision on, and encouraging them to generalise from these to other situations—rather than by starting from abstract concepts;

— *Active*—encouraging learners to learn by doing, rather than being told or preached at;

— *Relevant*—designing learning activities around real situations in the life of the school or college, the community or the wider world;

— *Collaborative*—employing group-work and co-operative learning;

— *Interactive*—teaching through discussion and debate ;

— *Critical*—encouraging learners to think for themselves, by asking for their opinions and views and helping them develop the skills of argument;

— *Participative*—allowing learners to contribute to their own learning, e.g., by suggesting topics for discussion or research, or by assessing their own learning or the learning of their peers.

The sorts of learning derive directly from the aim of EDC, and teachers need to become accomplished in employing them, e.g., knowing how to manage discussions and debates, organise group work, use different forms of questioning, and so on.

Management and People Skills

There are a number of different management and people skills that are required of the EDC teacher. These are seen most clearly in the following ways.

Creating an adequate learning climate

For effective EDC learning to take place teachers need to be able to create a climate that is non-threatening and enables everyone to speak freely and without ridicule. It is also important for the teacher to be able to ensure that the learning environment coheres or supports the intended learning objectives — in other words, that the 'medium matches the message'. For example, in a discussion on children's rights, students should be seated in a way that encourages them to listen and respond to one another on an equal basis — preferably in a circle. Similarly, freedom of expression must not only be understood as a principle of democracy, but practised in the classroom—suggesting student-centred methods of teaching.

Modelling skills and aptitudes, and values and dispositions

In EDC the teacher's personality is also part of the 'message'. EDC teachers need to learn how they can act as role models to demonstrate EDC skills—such as how to justify an opinion, or how to negotiate a consensus—or EDC dispositions—such as openness, or democratic leadership.

Dealing with controversial issues

EDC requires young people to share opinions and ideas on real-life issues that affect them and their communities. Issues of this kind can be controversial or sensitive, or both. EDC teachers, therefore, need to learn how they can encourage young people to speak their minds assertively while still respecting points of view different from their own. They also need to be aware of when they—as teachers—are entitled and not entitled to express their own views on a controversial issue.

Community beyond the classroom

The role of EDC in the education of young people extends far beyond the formal confines of the classroom. It also has a place in the life of the school as a whole and in the community outside the school. Young people learn how to become active citizens through being given a say in the running of the school and—in ways appropriate to their age—in taking responsibility for certain aspects of it. They also learn how to become active citizens through links made between the school and the wider community, e.g., through school or college councils, community events or campaigns. An important aspect of teacher training in EDC, therefore, is providing teachers with the expertise to be able to organise this dimension of EDC learning.

Reflection and Improvement Skills

The nature of EDC means that particular reflection and improvement skills are required in teachers.

Personal development

The need for self-reflection and for taking the time to pause, consider and draw lessons from experience and practice is to be fostered in teachers. Important aspects of self-reflection especially for EDC include the awareness of teachers' own values and dispositions and the coherence between these values and their EDC teaching and learning approaches. External or peer support can facilitate this process.

Professional development

On account of the dynamic nature of EDC and in order to ensure the relevance of EDC for students, regular updating and innovating of competences is required—in particular, EDC related knowledge as well as teaching and learning approaches.

Co-operation

Engaging in cooperative activity—i.e., acting and learning with and from others, particularly fellow teachers and other practitioners—contributes to teachers' personal and professional development as well as to improving their practice of EDC. Teamwork within the school, membership of an EDC-related professional association, networking at local, national or international level, European and international projects and exchanges are examples of this kind of co-operation.

12

ICTs in Teacher Training

Objectives of ICT Pre-service Programmes

The main objective of ICT pre-service teacher education programmes has been to produce teachers who:

(i) Are qualified and competent to employ the tools of the technology to supplement their traditional teaching methods and thereby achieve enhanced student learning,

(ii) Can use the tools of the technology to keep themselves abreast of the latest developments in the subject/s they teach, and

(iii) Can contribute to their own professional advancement.

After the training programme the prospective teachers are expected primarily to be able to

— Teach their subject/s using the tools of ICT wherever possible, achieving an appreciable degree of integration,

— Teach the basics of ICT, both theory and practice, that would enable their students to benefit from the tools of the technology,

— Employ and promote Web-based education as a strategy to promote directed self-learning among their students, and

— Motivate their students to pursue ICT in their future higher studies and as career options.

ICT Pre-service Training Policies

The National Council for Teacher Education (NCTE) is a statutory body constituted under an act of Parliament to regulate all aspects of teacher education in India. It played a pivotal role in the promotion of computer literacy among teacher educators during the early stages of introduction of an ICT component in the teacher education curriculum in the country. The NCTE also developed the curriculum guidelines and a suggested syllabus.

Almost all state and central government agencies have adopted a liberal policy of encouraging and supporting ICT curricula in pre-service teacher training institutions as recommended by the NCTE. A component of ICT in some form or other, and to different extents, is now an integral part of the teacher education curriculum for all students, either at the diploma level, which addresses the needs of elementary education, or at the degree level, which addresses the needs of secondary education. Some degree courses offer an entire paper on ICT as an elective subject and the number of institutions doing so is on the increase.

The teacher education curricula in ICT have been shaped to a significant extent by the document of the National Council of Educational Research and Training (NCERT) titled 'Information Technology in Schools—Curriculum Guide and Syllabus' which addresses the needs of the school system in the country. It also spells out the competencies required of both the students and teachers for transaction of the curriculum.

ICT Training for Elementary & Secondary Teachers

In most teacher training institutions no regular informatics course is offered to pre-service teacher trainees. Since the duration of the elementary training programme is two years as against one year for the secondary programme, it is not surprising that there is little difference between the ICT curricula for the two at present. However, till recently the elementary programme did not include any ICT component. There was only a component on audio-visual aids and equipment pertaining mainly to the pre-ICT era. As for ITC training for secondary teachers, the ICT related elective course, where offered, is more akin to an informatics course than the compulsory component.

ICT Training for Informatics & Non-informatics Teachers

At the mainstream school level, ICT training needs are of the non-Informatics type and as such, the conventional teacher training institutions focus largely on providing this type of training. However, polytechnics, technical schools and similar institutions that require teachers qualified in informatics courses such as Computer Science & Engineering meet their needs from among teachers trained by Technical Teachers Training Institutes (TTTIs) a number of which have been set up at the regional level by the government of India.

The training for informatics subject teachers is of a rigorous type involving in-depth studies of computer hardware, software, programming skills, digital electronics, mathematics, etc. The training for non-informatics subject teachers involves only the bare essentials of theory and practice. This includes learning to use common hardware such as PCs and their accessories, application and generic software, educational software resources, etc. The elective course available in some secondary teacher training institutions is of an intermediate variety.

Educational ICT usage in Training Programmes

Most teacher training institutions are equipped with a 'Computer Lab' consisting of 3 to 10 PCs, often of the outdated pre-Pentium variety, some peripheral devices such as dot matrix printer, TV, VCD player, some pre-installed generic application software, some multimedia educational software and a backup short duration power source. Overhead and slide projectors are also generally available. The usage of the facilities is mostly confined to the lab, occasionally extends to the seminar hall and very rarely to the classroom. Although a multimedia computer system is generally available, the much-needed LCD projector to go with it for mass viewing is still too expensive to afford.

Training Methodology

It is logical to expect that any training in ICT tools and techniques would be most effectives if it were done employing the very tools and techniques that are the subjects of teaching. However, the ground realities are different. The instructors do not employ these tools and techniques as often as the circumstances require and generally rely on the long established 'chalk and talk' lecture method, one that requires the least amount of preparation on their part. This happens even in institutions that have a good infrastructure and instructional facilities by way of commonly needed items of hardware, software and support material. It is not that the instructors lack the abilities and skills required for the purpose, but that they often prefer the easy, beaten track.

Distance Learning Systems

Some open universities such as the Indira Gandhi National Open University (IGNOU) offer pre-service secondary teacher education courses in the distance education mode. While they do employ a variety of electronic media, including TV broadcasts and Web-based programmes, much of the teaching-learning process still takes places through printed material exchanged through the national postal services and short duration contact programmes. The NCTE has laid down some stiff requirements and guidelines for such distance education programmes.

Duration of Programmes

The elementary pre-service teacher training programme used to be of one-year duration till recently, but it has been changed to a two-year course in almost all states on the initiative of the NCTE. Also, the entry qualification for students has been enhanced from matriculation to pre-university. Successful candidates are awarded a diploma (D Ed). The secondary pre-service teacher-training programme continues to be of one-year duration, with a university degree as the entry qualification.

The four regional institutes of education under the NCERT and a few university colleges offer a four-year integrated teacher education programme for which the entry qualification is pre-university. However, the number of students graduating from these courses is a very small fraction of those coming out of the system as a whole. The regional institutes of education have recently replaced their one-year programme by a more purposefully designed two-year programme.

The ICT components of the D Ed and B Ed courses vary widely from state to state and system to system. Some have only a notional representation in the overall curriculum while others have a strong and well-designed component. However, the courses are generally of the non-informatics type. Master degree programmes in education leading to the M Ed degree have also started introducing a component of ICT in their curriculum; some institutions also offer a more advanced version of it as an elective.

Teacher Educators

The NCTE has specified the minimum qualifications and, in certain cases, the prior experience required of the staff working in teacher education institutions throughout the country. Generally they should have a university master's degree in a school subject together with a master's degree in education (M Ed). They should preferably have some prior school teaching or teacher training experience. In the case of the head of the institution such experience is mandatory. These requirements came into effect after the establishment of the NCTE in the early ninetees. The NCTE has also prescribed that the student-teacher ratio in any programme has to be about 16:1.

When faced with the challenge of introducing ICT in the teacher education curricula most institutions were unprepared and most of the existing staff members very reluctant to taken on the additional responsibilities. Neither the infrastructure nor the human resources existed. It has taken more than a decade to remedy this situation and build up some level of basic resources.

In the last year or two there has been an explosive growth of teacher education institutions in the private sector, especially in the southern states. Hundreds of new institutions have come up despite the rather stringent norms set by the NCTE. It has not been easy for these new institutions to find teaching staff. As a result of the sudden spurt in demand, the quality of teacher educators in these institutions has suffered. Despite the impressive paper qualifications, the competence of teacher educators and hence the quality of teacher education have long been regarded as poor in the country, poorer than in any other sector of education.

Institutions catering to teacher education have generally been the slowest and most lukewarm in adapting to anything that is new and off the beaten track, especially to the demands of ICT in the revised teacher education curricula. This has severely affected the quality of teacher education in the country, with major repercussions on the quality of education imparted in schools and colleges. However, a younger generation of new entrants to the profession holds some promise for the future.

The situation with regard to (informatics) teacher trainers in Technical Teachers Training Institutions is a great deal more encouraging. They are generally engineering graduates, often in informatics subjects, well trained and motivated.

Elements of Teacher Education Programme

The non-informatics pre-service teacher education programme varies considerably from system to system and has basically the following content organised and sequenced in a variety of different ways:

- — Major developments in ICT in a chronological order
- — Concepts of hardware and software
- — Principal hardware components and peripherals of a multimedia and Internet-ready system
- — Distinction between system software and application software
- — Basics of WINDOWS operating environment
- — Essential programming concepts; but not the formal learning of any programming language except a simple graphics-oriented language like LOGO
- — Word processing, document preparation and printing
- — Spreadsheet applications, including graphical and statistical analysis of data
- — Fundamentals of database design, creation and management
- — Creation of multimedia presentations and slide shows using Power Point
- — Computer Aided Teaching & Learning
- — Interactive use of Multimedia educational software on CD-ROMs
- — Basic networking concepts, including the Internet
- — Using the Internet for e-mail and file transfer
- — Surfing the Internet for searching and selecting educational content and ideas for teaching The informatics programme also varies considerably from system to system and, in addition to all of the above components, has components like

— A detailed study of the operating system features
— A more in-depth study of hardware, peripherals and accessories
— Networking
— Computational Algorithms
— System Programming
— Application Programming
— Study of a structured programming language such as PASCAL, C or C++
— Object Oriented Programming concepts
— File Management
— Database Management
— Principles of Communications Technology
— Internet and Web Technology

Programme Development Initiatives

Initiatives for developments and reforms in ICT pre-service teacher education curricula can be traced directly or indirectly to various sources such as the NCTE, NCERT, the State Councils for Educational Research & Training (SCERTs), State Boards for School Education, Universities, TTTIs, etc. They are also influenced to some extent by developments in other countries. For example, the well-known CLASS (Computer Literacy and Studies in Schools) project initiated nationwide in the mid-eighties, which necessitated a large-scale in-service training of schoolteachers in Computer Education, was in collaboration with the UK government.

Private sector initiatives have also been playing a significant role in ICT training for teachers. Prominent among them are Intel's 'Teach to the Future' initiative nationwide and Microsoft's Project Shiksha in Maharashtra state. Intel's initiative is based on the conviction that '....all the educational technology is worth nothing if teachers don't know how to use it effectively'.

PROGRAMME PARTICIPANTS

There are thousands of teacher education institutions in the country with a student population of hundreds of thousands. The exact figures are uncertain because of the recent explosive growth of such institutions in the private sector. The NCTE approved student intake for the elementary course is 50 per section and for the secondary course 100 per section. A large number of institutions have been permitted to run more than one section for each course.

Pre-entry Qualification Requirements

The minimum qualification for the elementary course entrants is a pass in the class XII examination of state and centrals boards of school education. For the secondary course entrants, the minimum requirement is a university degree in any school subject. Selection is usually made through a common entrance examination conducted every year, generally at the state level.

Participant Performance during Training

Student performance during training is evaluated through a combination of formative and summative evaluation procedures. The evaluation is partly internal, through a process of continuous comprehensive evaluation, and partly external, through an annual external examination.

Post-programme Certification

At the end of a two-year programme of elementary teacher training the successful candidates qualify for a Diploma in Education (D Ed) in most states. At the end of a one-year programme of secondary teacher training the successful candidates qualify for a Bachelor's Degree in Education (B Ed) of the university to which the concerned institution is affiliated. A postgraduate one-year Master of Education (M Ed) course is also available in most university departments of education and other institutions.

Employment Opportunities and Salaries

For candidates with a diploma qualification, employment opportunities are mainly as teachers in elementary schools most of which are run by the state governments. Opportunities also exist as teachers in the elementary sections of central schools such as Kendriya Vidyalayas, Navodaya Vidyalayas, etc. For candidates with a degree in education, employment opportunities are mainly as teachers in government, governmentaided or private secondary schools. Opportunities also exit as teachers in the secondary sections of central schools. The NCTE has made these qualifications mandatory for all teachers.

Candidates with a master's degree in a school subject and a degree in education can become teachers in higher secondary schools at both the state and central levels. Candidates with an M Ed degree can become either teachers in secondary/higher secondary schools or teacher educators, either in the elementary or the secondary teacher education institutions.

Salaries paid to teachers and teacher educators vary widely from system to system and even from state to state. Teachers in government and government-aided elementary and secondary schools get a salary as prescribed by the concerned state government. Their counterparts in unaided private schools are paid salaries that are generally much lower and variable greatly from school to school. Only elite and reputed schools in the private sector pay salaries comparable to or more than government schools.

Salaries payable to teacher educators, whether in the government or private sector, are governed by NCTE regulations. Teacher educators in government run or government-aided institutions are paid salaries comparable to those paid to their counterparts in other colleges. In reality, salaries paid to teacher educators in privately managed teacher education institutions are significantly lower than the salaries paid in government and government-aided institutions.

On-the-job Performance

Mechanisms for appraisal of on-the-job performance of teachers and teacher educators do exist on paper but appear to be non-functional in practice. In effect, after the training phase, the performing teacher or teacher educator hardly ever gets evaluated in a regular and systematic manner. The system does little to discriminate between the effective and ineffective performance. There is also no effective reward / punishment mechanism.

Programme Providers

Role of Government and Private Sectors

Most of the early initiatives and financial support for the inclusion of ICT in teacher education programmes came from the Government of India and the state governments. The CLASS project that began in the mid eighties was the first major initiative in this regard, with technical support coming from the UK government. Government funds have been provided adequately for the development of ICT infrastructure and facilities in most government and government-aided institutions. Privately managed teacher training institutions have relied heavily on their own resources and support from non-governmental agencies.

IT enterprise giants such as Intel and Microsoft have provided substantial inputs into both schools and teacher training programmes selectively. Indian commercial IT enterprises such as NIIT (National Institute for Information Technology) have played a major role in creating infrastructure and human resources in some states such as Karnataka where a massive programme of providing Computer Education in secondary schools was initiated about a decade ago.

Stakeholder Participation

Stakeholder participation is confined mostly to government agencies and organisations and the managements of institutions in the private sector. Parents and community members who evince a fair amount of interest in school education, especially in the private sector, seem to show little or no interest in teacher education, though the parents pay considerable amounts of money to the managements of private institutions to get their wards admitted to the training courses.

Programme Quality

Accreditation Systems

All teacher education institutions in the country that conform to certain essential requirements and standards laid down by the NCTE are recognised by the NCTE to run teacher-training programmes. A component of ICT or separate courses in ICT related subjects have now become an integral part of the curricula in these programmes. The elementary teacher training institutions are affiliated to a designated board of education and examinations in their respective states. The secondary teacher training institutions are affiliated to a university under whose jurisdiction they come. The diplomas and degrees awarded to their outgoing students are valid and recognised for purposes of employment throughout the country.

Standards

Standards with regard to infrastructure, instructional facilities, entry-level requirements, teacher educator qualifications, etc., have been established by the NCTE and generally accepted by all stakeholders. The examining boards and universities implicitly set student performance standards. Provision for periodic revision/renewal of teacher education curricula, including the ICT components, ensures conformity with changing scenarios and global developments.

Costs & Funding Responsibilities

In government teacher education institutions the entire running costs, nearly 95% of which goes towards staff salaries, are met by the government. The government also meets capital expenditure, including expenditure towards setting up of ICT facilities. A small fraction of the overall expenditure is recovered through student fees, which are nominal.

In government-aided institutions the general practice is for the government to meet the entire expenditure towards staff salaries and other costs are expected to be met from student fees and institutional resources. Privately managed institutions depend heavily upon student fees and institutional resources to meet both the staff salaries and running costs. Generally, no separate distinction is made in respect of the costs of procurement and maintenance of ICT hardware and software. Private institutions often charge a separate fee from students towards the capital expenditure on ICT infrastructure.

Programme Sustainability

In government and government-aided teacher education institutions the sustainability of the ICT programme is not in doubt since the government bears practically all the costs and the demand for admission to these institutions is high. However, the question of sustainability is a pertinent one in privately managed institutions since the resources have to be raised mainly through student fees and these are generally high.

Only those students who cannot get into the government supported institutions generally end up in private institutions, incurring high costs. In view of the recent explosive growth of teacher training institutions in the private sector, especially in the southern region, and the lowering demand for admission to privately managed institutions, the long term sustainability of the programme in such institutions is definitely in question.

Bibliography

Beegle, Charles W.; Brandt, Richard M., eds. "Observational Methods in the classroom". Washington, D.C.: Association for Supervision and Curriculum Development, 1973.

Beyer, Landon E. and others. "Preparing Teachers as Professionals". New York: Teachers College Press, 1989.

Broderick, Maria, editor. "For Teachers about Teaching". *Cambridge: Harvard Educational Review,* 1988.

Burke, Peter. "Teacher Development: Induction, Renewal, and Redirection". New York: Falmer Press, 1987.

Darling-Hammond, Linda, editor. "Professional Development Schools: Schools for Developing a Profession". New York: Teachers. College Press, 1994.

Dollase, Richard H. "Voices of Beginning Teachers: Visions and Realities". New York: Teachers College Press, 1992.

Dunkin, Michael J. "International Encyclopedia of Teaching and Teacher Education". Oxford: Pergamon Press, 1987.

Goble, Norman M.; Porter, James F. "The Changing Role of the Teacher: International Perspectives". Paris: UNESCO, 1977.

Goodings, Richard; Byram, Michael Byram; McPartland, Michael, eds. *Changing Priorities in Teacher Education.* London: Croom Helm, 1982.

Hare, William. "What Makes a Good Teacher: Reflections on Some Characteristics Central to the Educational Enterprise". London, ONT: Althouse Press, 1993.

Myers, Douglas; Reid, Fran, eds. Educating Teachers: Critiques and Proposals. Toronto: Ontario Institute for Studies in Education, 1974.

Pearson, Allen T. *The Teacher: Theory and Practice in Teacher Education*. New York: Routledge, 1989.

Peters, R.S. *Education and the Education of Teachers*. London, Routledge & Kegan Paul, 1977.

Tulasiewics, Witold; Adams, Anthony, editors. *Teachers Expectations and Teaching Reality*. London: Routledge, 1989.

Index